I can't hear the birds anymore.

By Brenda Portwood

A true story about survival against all odds.

WARNING: The contents of this book contain graphic descriptions of abuse, and its horrific results. It is intended to educate caregivers, and the abused themselves about what really happened, and how to detect it.

If you believe that you, or someone you know has been abused, please get professional help immediately. Most areas have a confidential abuse hotline.

Disclaimer: Several of the people's names and/or relationships have been changed in the telling of the story, also a few locations have not been named for personal reasons. These changes have not altered the events and what had happened in them.

Wholesale: Quantity discounts are available on bulk purchases of this book for reselling, educational resources, gifts or fundraising. For more information please contact the Author at:
Spirit Creek Publishing, (780) 964-3123.

ACKNOWLEDGEMENTS

I would like to thank the following people, for without their support, encouragement and understanding this story would never have been told:

To Bud,
For choosing to share your life with me and wanting to go on this journey. You believed in me from the very beginning. You loved me and knew who I was before I did. I thank you from the bottom of my heart for standing with me through it all.

To my two daughters,
For being an anchor to my soul and for giving me a reason to survive it all.

To Dr. L. Brooks,
For having the foresight to point me in the right direction.

To Lorraine
(Kukui Fountainhead Retreat),
For helping me to open up Pandora's Box and survive.

To all my horses:
The time we spent together during those horrible years will never be forgotten.

Without all of you in my life helping me to survive,
I am not sure where I would be today.

I would like to give a special thanks to:

Tracy Hustler for the Author's photo.

Eveline Garneau for the illustration and for putting what was
in my head onto paper for the cover of the book.

Andrew for encouraging me to go with the title.

Kathleen and Coralie for being encouraging and excited about
this project.

My dad, for understanding and accepting why I needed to
write this book.

This is not a story about revenge.
This is not a story about pity or blame.
This is not a story about a victim.

This is a story about a five year old little girl.
This is a story about a survivor.

This is a story about a little girl who found someone who
believes her and will protect her forever:
Herself.

This is a story about a little girl and her struggle
to gain her life back.

Her story needs to be told so that other victims/survivors can gain
the courage to stand up and take back control of their lives.
This is a story about a woman who is finding her life.
This is a story about Choices.

She was dead, but her eyes were open and she was breathing.

Her eyes were deep pools of sadness. If someone could have looked into her eyes, they would have been able to see her soul, and they would have become lost in the depth of despair, betrayal and isolation that had started to grow there, like a cancer.

Her eyes were sad and lifeless.
They were the eyes of someone who had died, but was still living.

This little girl was five.

Table of Contents

Acknowledgements iii

Prologue 1

Chapter One 3
   ... Cocoa 3
   ... the day my life changed 8
   ... frozen with fear 17
   ... the beginning of "why"????? 19
   ... can't get away... 21
   ... the death of a spirit 25
   ... possible excuses 31
   ... survival 33

Chapter Two 35
   ... the bear 35
   ... egg shampoo 38
   ... lonely grade two 40
   ... the lease, finding my peace 42
   ... our neighbours 45
   ... Sailor 48
   ... a baby?????... 50
   ... 1969 51
   ... Father Gender, the priest 54

Chapter Three 57
   ... hitchhiking 57
   ... I am leaving 59
   ... the leather strap 62
   ... my saviours 67
   ... the loners 78

Chapter Four 81
   ... the memory 81
   ... loneliness 84
   ... 1970, the end of the baby 87
   ... never again 90
   ... am i finally saved?... 95

Chapter Five 101
  … has God finally sent me my relief? …...................101
  … was it a coincidence or a premonition? … 103
  … don't trust them … 106
  … he seems different …...109
  … he seems nice and safe ….......................................111
  … trying to escape …...114
  … leave me alone … 119
  … I give up …...121
  … warning lights - I think … 123

Chapter Six 125
  … the dress …..125
  … 1976, my new life …..129
  … meaning …..132
  … later, reality sets in …..135

Chapter Seven...139
  … trust no one with your children ….........................139
  … Wheezy, the "Hell" woman ….................................142
  … little things …..147
  … the tote bag … 150
  … the nightmare …..154
  … broken trust …..156

Chapter Eight..159
  … the beginning of a new life ….................................159
  … moving on alone … 161
  … hiding the horses …..169
  … Joyous Noel, not so joyous …................................177
  … saving Arion … 179
  … a death, and a murder contract ….........................183
  … seeking help …...185
  … "oh my God" it's really true … 193

Epilogue..201

About The Author: 205

PROLOGUE

When I first started to write this book, I thought that I would be able to stand outside of the memories of my abuse. I thought that I would be able to talk about the memories in the past tense.

I thought that I would be able to narrate what was happening in the images that showed in my mind and not get involved in them.

I was wrong

When I started to tell the story about the sexual abuse I endured that had started at age five, I became that five year old again.

I started to talk like I talked when I was five. I did not remember how to spell simple words, let alone larger ones. My grammar was that of a five year old child and so were my perceptions.

The five year old child was channeling through me: I was her vessel. I had no choice but to sit there in front of my computer and type everything she said, and everything that she felt. Every sexual and abusive attack came tumbling forward, every emotion.

As the story came pouring out, the memories became clearer. Things that I could not say out loud came stumbling out onto the keyboard. I was telling the story for the first time, unedited.

I could not type as fast as she was speaking. Her words were running out of me, and I would have to try and slow her down so that I could keep up with what she was saying. I wanted to get the memories down correctly and accurately for her.

My subconscious mind had taken over and there was no turning back. When I had finished typing her memories, I could not read them. I found the memories too graphic and the emotions too raw.

At that time, even as an adult, I could not say parts of the memories out loud. I was not sure how the little girl handled it all.

After I finished putting the memories down on paper, I was emotionally drained. I noticed that the weight on my shoulders had changed: it felt lighter; I could breathe easier; and I was starting to feel more of an inner peace flowing.

After a while, I printed off a copy of the memories and gave them to my confidante, Lorraine. With her help, I have been able to break through the black wall that had surrounded me and isolated me for so long. I don't think that even Lorraine was prepared for the rest of the details of the memories that had flooded out on the paper.

I am so glad that I survived the traumatic events that had happened when I was little. I am so thankful that I was there for the little girl in me. To me, she was someone special.

Her story needs to be told.

I have noticed throughout the progression of the book that I was the five year old little girl, but I was also the adolescent, the teenager, and the young woman that the events happened to. I have continued to be their typist, their friend and their confidante while they all told me their memories. I have never once questioned them about the abuse or their memories.

This is their story. This is my story.

CHAPTER ONE

I was a happy child with a very independent streak. The first five years of my life were, I assume like every child's life, filled with playing and getting dirty. Everything changed the summer of my fifth year.

... Cocoa ...

Little did I know that my dog and many horses would became my saviours during the rough times in my childhood and youth. Without them I don't know where I would have ended up. They anchored me to the present and helped me hide from the past. Unfortunately they did not have the ability to help me forget or deal with the abuse, but they did save me nonetheless.

My Dad owned a bay mare named "Cocoa." I loved Cocoa and like many young girls, I was horse crazy. I wanted to ride all of the time. I probably drove Dad crazy with my constant yammering about it.

One warm spring day, after Dad had finished checking on the cows in the field with Cocoa, he was standing in the garage unsaddling her. I was there, as usual, wanting to ride her. Finally he must have gotten fed up with my constant nagging and told me that if I could get on her all by myself then I could have her as my very own horse.

He told me that I could not have any help: no help with a stool, no saddle, nothing. Dad then dropped the reins of her bridle to the ground and walked to the house.

I think Dad underestimated my determination. I am sure he did not think that I would be able to get on. Never underestimate a very determined five year old. Cocoa was a very patient horse, actually she probably was happy to just stand there in the garage in the shade and sleep.

I stood there for a long time sizing her up. Boy was she huge! If I stood in front of Cocoa I could just touch the bottom part of her neck with my head.

I tried to crawl up Cocoa's front legs, then I tried to run up to her side and jump on her back but these attempts always resulted in me landing on my butt on the floor. No matter how many times I landed on my butt, I would keep trying the same way.

After becoming very tired, I gave up and just sat down on the floor. I sat there staring at the horse and wondering, *how am I ever going to get on her?*

One important thing about Cocoa was that she had a really beautiful long brown mane. If I stood on my tiptoes, I could grab hold of some of the hair. As I sat there staring at her, I had a great idea. I would crawl up her mane.

This plan would only work if Cocoa put her head down enough so that I could grab the hair just behind her ears. So I waited.

Finally Cocoa mistakenly let her head down and "bam" I had her hair. Just as fast as I grabbed her mane she threw up her head. There I was hanging there, dangling in the wind.

Now what?

I tried using her hair like you would use monkey bars, hanging on with one hand and grabbing another handful of hair further down her mane. This method was working until I got closer to her back. Then I just hung there. I could not get my skinny legs up high enough to even touch her backbone.

I guess she finally got tired of me hanging there and put her head down again. I promptly lost my grip and dropped to the floor.

Well so much for that idea.

Cocoa refused to put her head down low enough so that I could grab her the mane close to her head again.

I stood dejectedly under her neck, thinking *I am never going to be able to ride, I can't get on her.*

I was almost ready to give up when I turned and buried my head into her chest and stretched my arms up to hug the large part of her neck. As I stood there hugging her neck I started to play with a piece of her mane that I could grab. I was feeling sorry for myself.

All good things happen in time and this time was no different. Suddenly my brain kicked into gear, *Wait, I can feel her mane!*

While hugging her and playing with her hair a great idea had formed.

I turned around and grabbed that small clump of mane with my left hand, then I pressed my back into her front legs, with all my strength I ran, my left hand hanging on to her mane and my right arm stretched out as far as it would go, my toes digging into the dirt as I ran a semi-circle. My right hand was ready to grab more mane after I jumped.

On the first attempt I made it halfway up her side. I tried again and again and again. With each jump I was able to jump a little higher. Finally on the second last try I was able to get my leg up high enough to get my toes to touch her back.

I thought: *Almost there; run faster, jump harder, jump higher.*

On the last jump I was finally able to get my toes over her backbone. So there I was, hanging off of her side, like a monkey hanging onto a branch. Cocoa was not impressed with this new development and promptly put her head up high in the air. When she did that her backbone dropped down and I was able to gain the last few inches.

Now I was squirming up Cocoa's side, using her mane as a rope, my right leg stretched up to her backbone, my toes hanging on. I had renewed vigor and was not going to let go. Cocoa still was not impressed and snorted and held her head high in the air. I kept squirming and wriggling until I finally made it. Wow, I was sitting on her back and I had gotten on her all by myself! I sat there for a while feeling rather proud of myself for getting on her. Cocoa was my horse now.

My heart was beating wildly, my eyes were sparkling and I had an ear-to-ear grin on my face.

I thought, *WOW, I have to show Dad that I got on her all by myself!* But wait, the reins were still hanging down from her bridle. Cocoa was ground-tied and would not move. My arms were too short to reach the bridle, so instead I stuck my foot out for her to see, and when she turned her head to smell my toes, I grabbed hold of the side of her bridle. Then I slid my hand down until I was able to grab the reins. Well, one rein.

One rein was going to have to do, so I kicked her and we walked proudly out of the garage and into the yard and stopped in front of the house.

Dad came out of the house, looked at me and with a big smile, handed me the other rein and said, "Well, now that she is yours you are going to have to take care of her."

I don't think you could have gotten a bigger smile on my face.

Dad asked me how I had gotten on her, so I told him. Then he asked if I would show him how. So with much zeal, I promptly slid off Cocoa, positioned myself under her neck and flew.

I can safely say that I surprised my dad that day.

Getting on Cocoa was not always easy, especially if she decided that she did not want to go on another adventure with me. Sometimes when I would try "The Jump" to get on her she would drop her head down. When she did that, I would slide right down her neck on my belly and fall off.

In the following weeks, months and years to come, Cocoa would become my escape, my confidante and my steed that would take me away from all the bad things. She was destined to be my saviour.

We spent endless hours together having many great and exciting adventures. We also had many not so happy adventures. Instead of having fun with her, I would be on the lookout for new places for me to hide.

I am forever grateful for Cocoa's loyalty and the protection that she provided me in my youth. In all the years we spent together, Cocoa never hurt a hair on my head. She was such an amazing horse.

Angels and protectors come into one's life in many ways. Cocoa was the first of many to come into my life.

... the day my life changed ...

In 1955, Mom and Dad had moved to a little Hamlet in rural Northern Alberta with hopes of building a new life and a home for their family. You could purchase a homestead under the condition that you had to have a large number of acres of the bush land cleared each year and put into crops. By the time Mom and Dad moved their house onto the property from the rental land, Dad had cleared enough bush for our yard site and the house Dad had built to sit on it.

It was 1962, our house was a small two bedroom house for the six of us, with a living room, kitchen and eating area in one. There was a small porch in the front. We did not have running water, which was not put in until I was about 13 years old. We did have a black and white TV with one channel, and we had a radio with a record player. My brothers slept in one room and Mom and Dad and I slept in the other.

The yard was huge. There was no grass to speak of, only dirt, and boy did we get dirty. There were a row of trees on the east and west side of the yard that protected it from the wind. Dad had built a garage for all his tools and equipment on the northeast side of the house. Behind the garage was the backyard where the barn and corrals were for the cattle, and the chicken coop for the chickens as well as a small pig pen for piglets. A bigger pig pen was on the other side of the trees on the east side of the yard. On the other side of the trees, on the west side, was a pasture for the cows and Cocoa.

It was a hot and beautiful spring day. The sun was shining. There wasn't any breeze to help cool us down. I loved the warmth of those hot days. While everyone was in the field or working in the backyard, I would play in all the dirt that surrounded the house, making horse trails and hills for my imaginary horses to run on. Soon the grass seed that Dad had sown would grow and we would have a lawn to play on.

It was a peaceful outside. I could heard all the birds singing their chirping songs as I played around the house and by the trees. I imagined them singing sweet melodies to each other like the songs my mom and dad listened to every Sunday morning. It was so peaceful listening to all the birds. I would lay on the ground under the trees and float away on their beautiful sounds. I loved the sound of all the different noises in the songs that they sang, it was magic to hear.

It was lunch time, and Mom was making sandwiches for everyone. She called me in from outside to set the table and get ready to eat. Dad, my three older brothers, and Ted the farm hand, were all sitting around the kitchen table waiting for their lunch. Everyone was talking and laughing, having a good time. I remember they each looked funny with dirt all over their faces from working in the field. Even Mom had dirt on her face. I was happy.

When lunch was finished, Mom quickly washed the dishes and asked me to dry them while she went back out into the field with everyone else. While I was alone in the house drying the dishes, Ted came back and sat on the couch for a while bugging me. I did not like him. He kept talking stupid and I did not understand what he was saying.

Ted was 18 or 19 years old. He was a tall and very skinny person. His brown hair had been cut off very short with a razor, like my mom used to cut my brothers' hair. He had a long and skinny face with a big long nose. His teeth were dirty and crooked. I remember that he had very big ears and smelled awful.

While I stood at the counter drying the dishes, he undid his pants and pulled out his peter. It was big. I had seen my brothers' peters when they had to take off their clothes to have a bath in the big tub that mom would set up in the living room beside the heater.

He then started rubbing his peter. While rubbing it he told me he wanted me to come over and feel it, but I did not want to. When I refused, he got off the couch and took several strides to where I was standing, grabbed my arm and dragged me back to the couch. I started to yell for help and yelled at him to let me go. He just laughed and told me that no one could hear me because they had all left to go back out into the fields to work. He said that he had come back just to see me.

I was trying to get away, but he wrapped his legs around my waist and squeezed so hard that I could hardly move or breathe. He held my hands with one hand, and with the other hand shoved my face downwards.

When the abuse was over, he loosened his legs from around my waist. I fell to the floor, gagging, and crawled away. I sobbed "I'm going to tell my Dad!"

Ted got off the couch, walked over and grabbed me by my arm. He held me up in the air shaking me by my arm. He took out his knife and pointed the blade at my shoulder.

"If you ever tell anyone, I'll kill your Mom and Dad" Ted sneered. "Everyone will know that you are a bad girl, and that you killed them." He asked what kind of girl would I be, and said that everyone would hate me and I would be all by myself, that no one would ever want me if they knew.

He said that my Mom and Dad would not believe me. Then he said, "Who would believe you, if they were all dead?"

Then he told me that he would chop me up and then put me in the slop pail and feed me to the pigs.

He ordered me to finish drying the dishes, and then he left the house, slamming the screen door after him.

I stayed laying on the floor in the living room area crying. I didn't know what to do. My whole body was shaking and it was hard to try to even stand. I was confused and did not understand what had happened. My only thought was: "I am going to tell Dad on him."

Slowly the shaking subsided a bit and I was able to get up off the floor. I could not finish the dishes. I had to get out of the house, before he came back.

I could hear the tractor running out in the backyard. I ran over there to tell Dad what Ted had done. When I got to the tractor, Ted was standing there behind Dad. When he saw me, he took his knife out of his pocket and pointed it at Dad's back. Then he licked his lips and blew me a kiss while rubbing his crotch. I ran back to the yard and hid.

I hid in our dog Sandy's doghouse beside the house. I was so scared that Ted was going to come back to the house. I was scared that he had hurt Dad with his knife. I did not know what to do! I didn't know if Dad was okay. I stayed in Sandy's doghouse, crying, too scared to come out.

It was hot in the dog house. Spiders and bugs were crawling everywhere. There were spiders' webs in all the corners of the roof; spiders dangling there waiting for their next meal. I would try to brush the ones that were crawling in the straw near me away, but they kept crawling back to me so I pushed myself as far back I could get in Sandy's doghouse and piled the straw that we used for his bed in front of me. I could hardly breathe. The air was so hot and stuffy.

Everything outside of the doghouse was quiet. I could not hear the tractor running. I could not hear anyone. I couldn't hear the birds anymore. All I listened for was Ted's footsteps. I was totally alone.

I realized that I could never tell Mom or Dad what Ted did. I was afraid that he would stab them with his knife. I wasn't really sure what "kill" meant, but the way Ted had said it, and the way he pointed his knife at Dad's back, had made me scared.

Later that day Mom came back into the house. After she had gone into the house, I peeked my head out of Sandy's doghouse to see if I could see Ted anywhere. When I thought that it was okay, I crawled out and ran into the house where Mom was.

That night before supper was ready, I crawled up on Dad's lap and sat there for a while. He asked me what I had been doing all day. I told him that I had been in Sandy's doghouse, then I asked Dad what the word "kill" meant.

He said: "That is when you make something die, and then it goes away to heaven."

I asked him: "Do you get to see it again?"

"No. Why do you want to know?"

I did not say anything, instead I just laid my head on his shoulder. Dad asked me if I was okay and I mumbled, "Yes."

I was scared of Ted. I did not want him to kill Dad. I did not want Dad to go away.

Mom had put the large pot on the stove to heat water for washing the supper dishes. While waiting for the water to heat, I helped by clearing off the table, putting things away and stacking the dirty dishes. When the water was hot enough, Mom started washing the dishes and putting the clean dishes in a pan for drying. She told me to grab the tea towel and help dry the dishes. As I was standing there with the tea towel in my hand, I suddenly started to feel sick to my stomach. My hands started shaking, and pretty soon my legs also started to tremble. Standing at the counter shaking, I looked at Mom and said that I wanted to go and lay down on my bed. I said that I was tired and was not feeling very good, that I had a tummy ache. Mom looked at me and said "Okay," then she called Hank and Al to come over and help dry the dishes for her.

I headed off to the bedroom that I shared with Mom and Dad. My small bed was located against the outside wall of the house. I had to walk past the curtained closet, dresser and the window that was located directly opposite Mom's and Dad's bed to reach mine.

I lay down and held my big stuffed blue dog in my arms. My stuffed dog was as tall as I was and he sat on his hind end in a begging position. He slept with me every night at the foot of my bed, but tonight I wrapped my little arms around him, buried my face into the back of his head and hugged him tightly.

I was lying on my left side facing the curtain door of the bedroom. I could see Dad sitting on the couch in the living room. He was reading a book; Dad liked to read western books. As I lay there watching Dad, I was getting scared. I did not want Ted to kill Dad, I did not want my dad to go away to heaven and never to see him again. Tears started to roll out of the corners of my eyes and rolled across my nose and into my left ear.

Al and Hank were not happy that they had to help Mom with the dishes, I heard them both whine that doing dishes was girls' work. Al was a year and a half older than me and Hank three years older than me.

As I lay there sobbing with my head bent pressing into the back of my dog's head, I heard footsteps at the bedroom door. I moved my head slightly so that I could peek over the top of my dog's head and saw Al get down on his hands and knees and slowly sneak into the bedroom, I closed my eyes and listened to him crawling along the bedroom floor. When he got right beside my bed he reached up and grabbed my blue stuffed dog and tried to yank it out of my arms. I lay there with my eyes closed, hanging onto my dog. I hung on tightly and when Al could not pull the dog out of my arms he started to holler to Mom that I was faking it and I was not sleeping. Mom told him to leave me alone and to get back there to help with the dishes. I peeked my eyes open when I heard Al stomp off to the kitchen. I stayed in my bed the rest of the night.

A few days later Dad and Ted were in the back yard beside the pig pen. I was walking over to see Dad, and I did not see the Ted standing on the other side of Dad. But he had seen me. He stepped out from behind Dad, bent over at the waist and suddenly started to run toward me. I started to scream and ran back the way I had come.

As I was running and screaming, Ted was grabbing at my bum and snorting like a pig. Dad was laughing and Ted was laughing too. Finally Dad told him to quit bugging me.

When Ted quit chasing me, he stood up and turned to walk back to where Dad was. I was mad at my Dad for laughing at me and I was mad at Ted. I was so angry and hurt, I picked up a rock and threw it at Ted. The rock hit him on the side of his head. He grabbed his head, yelling and swearing.

When Dad heard him yelling, he stopped what he was doing and turned around. Dad was not smiling any more. He stomped over to me, grabbed me by my arm and hit my butt, then he marched me over to Ted and told me to say that I was sorry. I was crying and mad at both of them. I refused to tell Ted that I was sorry.

Ted bent his big ugly head down close to me, and looked at me and said: "Don't you have something to say to me?"

I looked at him. He had a nasty smile on his face. He scared me, so I told him that I was sorry, even though I did not feel bad for what I did.

I could not understand why Dad had laughed at me and why he was mad at me. I thought that Ted was right, nobody would believe me if I told them what he did to me, they would laugh at me. Nobody cared about me, they only cared about stupid Ted.

Sometimes if I was walking past the pig pen, Ted would sneak up behind me and grab me. He would wrap his arm around my waist and carry me like a sack of potatoes to the pig pen and pretend to throw me in. I would scream and kick. Then I would start to cry and beg him not to feed me to the pigs. Ted would laugh a sick perverted laugh. He seemed to be enjoying it.

One time he leaned over the fence of the pen and put me down beside the big pigs. I stared to scream and kick at the pigs. He told me that if I kept screaming, the pigs would get mad and start to eat me. So I stood there shaking and crying, hoping and praying that the pigs would not bite me. The whole time he forced me to stand in the pen he held onto my arms. Ted ordered me to look at him. I raised my head and tried to look at him, but he looked all fuzzy.

I could feel the pigs sniffing my legs and pushing at me. My heart was pounding so hard that I could hear it in my ears. Every time I turned my head to look down at the pigs, he would shake me and tell me to look at him and not the pigs.

I was crying and begging him to take me out of the pen. I told him that the pigs were going to bite me. I was so scared. He said he wanted the pigs to smell me, so that if he had to feed me to them they would know that it was me they were eating. He said that if I told anyone "the secret," then he would let the pigs eat me. I shook my little head back and forth and I told him, "No, I won't ever tell, I promise, Please don't let the pigs eat me!"

When Ted was satisfied that he had scared me enough into not telling, he lifted me out of the pig pen. But before he let me go, he took his dirty hanky out of his pocket and wiped my face with it. It was gross. He had boogers on it.

After that day, I avoided the pig pens as much as possible. If the pigs were in their pens, I was okay, but if the pigs got out, I was terrified that they would eat me. I was not afraid of the baby pigs, I was bigger than them. But I was very afraid of the big pigs. Ted said that if I got too close to them or if they got loose they would eat me.

I tried to stay away from Ted as much as possible. I started to hide in different places on the farm and sneak through the bushes so that he could not see me. I would watch Ted, with Dad and my older brother working in the yard. They would be laughing and having fun.

I did not understand why Dad was laughing with Ted. How could he talk to him?

I felt so sad, lonely and defeated. I did not know what I had done to make Ted hurt me. I only knew that I had to hide from him.

While writing this story and re-reading it, I can feel an overwhelming wave of desperation and sadness for that young girl. I can still see her tear-stained, confused little face looking out from behind the bushes, watching Ted and her dad. Wishing she could run out of her hiding place and yell at her dad that Ted was bad, that he had hurt her! But she was afraid that nobody would believe her. I can feel my chest getting heavy. It is hard to breathe.
I am that five year old terrified little girl again.

... frozen with fear ...

Later in the fall, Dad decided that it was time to butcher some of the big pigs before winter set in. This was a common practice among homesteaders to provide meat during the long winter months. We also ate vegetables from the garden that were being stored in root cellars.

I was standing in the backyard when one of the big male pigs came through the trees from the pig pen. I did not remember that they had turned the pig out so that Dad could shoot it.

My heart was pounding. I stood there frozen behind Dad not able to move, terrified that the pig would see me. Dad aimed his gun at the pig and shot, but the pig did not fall down. Instead it started to run toward me. Dad shot again.

All that I remember is being so scared that I could not move. Life around me had stopped. The pig was heading straight for me. I was going to be eaten by the pig! I was shaking, and my mind was screaming for my body to move. But nothing would move. I could not even scream. At the moment there was only me and that giant wild pig with fangs hanging out of its mouth, snorting and squealing and coming straight at me!

The pig died after the second shot. It fell to the ground with blood running out of its mouth and nose.

Dad had killed the pig. And saved me. My mind slowly began to comprehend what really had happened, Dad did not save me.

Dad had shot the pig for us to eat. I could see the tractor was coming to pick up the pig and then they put it in a barrel full of hot water so that they could scrape off the hair before they cut the pig apart into pieces.

... the beginning of "why"????? ...

When I got older, I could not understand why I was so terrified of pigs. I did not remember anything that Ted had done to me regarding the pigs until years later.

I guess your mind does strange things to help protect you from horrible memories. Mine had left small fragments of memories floating just out of my reach. I hoped one day to be able to unlock those images and begin to understand why I was so afraid.

When I was older, all of the family would go to the local Auction Market for the cattle, horse, sheep and pigs sales. Before the sale would start, I would make myself walk down the aisle of pens holding the big pigs that were to be auctioned off that day. I did this in hopes of trying to conquer the strange uneasiness I felt around them. I would even lean over their pens and touch them.

When some of them would start to squeal or fight, my heart would start racing and I could hardly breathe. I would freeze and became unable to walk past the pig pens. I was terrified that they would get out of their pens and attack me. I felt so stupid. I could not understand why I was so scared.

When it was time for the pigs to go into the sale ring, I made sure that I was not in the alleyway. No matter how hard I tried, I could not stay in the back where the pens were when the men started to chase the pigs.

I would sit in the stands above the sale ring on the very top row, watching, feeling safe but frightened, and angry with myself for being so stupid. I thought that I was such a baby, being afraid of the pigs.

I never told anyone that I was afraid. I did not want anyone to force me to go around them. I knew that if my brothers knew they would scare me all the time with the pigs and I did not want that.

As I was growing up, I never had any fear of any of the other livestock on the farm, just the pigs.

... can't get away...

Whenever I could, I tried to stay away from Ted and the farm. I would hide in the bushes that lined our yard or sneak out to the field to catch Cocoa and take her on all-day rides

When Ted arrived at the farm to work in the field for Dad, the minute I figured I knew where Ted was, I would head off to the corral to catch Cocoa and disappear for the day.

On this one particular day, Cocoa was standing in the cattle shelter out of the hot sun. I had already put on her bridle and was going to leave the farm because Ted had come there to work for dad again. But before I could get away, Ted found me.

He must have seen me going to the corral to catch her. He snuck up behind me and cornered me in the cattle shelter with Cocoa.

Ted was supposed to be on his way out to the field to finish ploughing or something. He told me that he would give me 50 cents if I would let him lick me. I told him to leave me alone. He threw his head back and started to laugh, I quickly crawled under Cocoa's belly to get to the other side of her so that Ted could not grab me. Then I heard Dad yelling for him. When Ted turned his back to yell back to Dad that he was heading his way, I jumped on Cocoa's back and took off. I left him standing in the shelter.

For days after that Ted hunted me like a dog. I was not so lucky the next time he found me.

Everyone was busy hauling in straw bales from the field and stacking them up for winter. I loved lying on the very top of the straw stack watching the clouds drift by. No one would see me on the top of the stack if they walked by, but if they were in the field then they could see me laying up there. I used to lie there staring at the clouds really hard until a shape would take form: it could be a boat, a rabbit, a galloping horse or even a dragon. I would spend hours laying there daydreaming and watching the clouds go by. From the top of the stack I could also see the field and where everybody was. I would know where Ted was.

One particular day I headed to my favorite hiding place on the top of the straw stack. When I got to the stack, I noticed that some bales had been moved around and placed in the shape of a fort without a roof. The bales had been piled three high on three sides with the open side facing the rest of the stack. As I stood there looking at the fort, Ted snuck up behind me and grabbed me by the arm. His pants were undone and he had a sick look in his eyes.

I tried to get my arm free, but his grip was stronger than mine. He pushed me down onto the ground in the straw fort. With one hand he held my wrists together; with the other he pulled my pants and panties down.

I screamed and kicked my legs as hard as I could. My heart was pounding so hard that I thought it was going to burst. I could hardly breathe. I had to get away! I tried to pull my hands free, but I could not, so I tried to bite him. He started to laugh and told me that my bites felt like little mosquitoes' bites. I hated him.

My bottoms were pulled down to my ankles. I was trying to kick him but he held my legs still with his shoulder and the other hand. Then he pinned my right leg down with his legs and used his left shoulder to try and spread my legs apart, but could not because my pants were in the way. I screamed at him to leave me alone, but all he did was laugh. He told me to scream all I wanted, that nobody was around to hear me. Then he said the more I screamed the more he liked it and the more he wanted me. I quit screaming but the tears kept running down the sides of my face. Then he crawled on top of me. I could hardly breathe he was so heavy. He started to rub his body all over me, licking my skin and moaning and dripping spit all over me. His shirt was open and I could feel his sweaty skin on me and the buckle of his belt was biting into my legs.

When it was over his breathing was fast and he whispered hoarsely in my ear that he had enjoyed himself and that I should feel special because he was the only one who loved me and was not afraid to show it. He said he knew that I liked it too and that I should not hide from him anymore. He said that he could not wait until we were together again.

I did not like it and I wished he would leave me alone.

I turned to look at his face, inches from mine, I could see his brown crooked teeth and I could smell his ugly breath. I started to gasp from the smell. I swallowed hard to stop from throwing up all over my clothes. I told him that I didn't care that nobody loved me. I told him that I hated him. He then grabbed my face, pinching my cheeks together and told me not to lie to him, that he would not treat me so special if I did not behave. He said he would have to hurt me more if I did not behave. Then he said to me that he had to be patient. I was not sure what he meant by that.

When he finally moved off of me, he looked at his thing and said, "You make me so horny and I can tell that you want me to. You like to play hide and seek, but I always find you because you want me to. Don't you?" Then he said, "Then next time we get together is going to be really special."

I could hear the tractor coming back. My mind was racing, *Thank God someone is coming.* And then: *Oh no, he will kill them! Oh no, they will know that I was bad!*

Ted quickly grabbed his pants and pulled them on, then told me to pull my pants up and to get to the house.

I was never so glad to run away in all my life. I hated Ted and never wanted to see him again. When I got to the trees, I turned around to see him moving the bales around so that the fort was gone. Then he pretended to be stacking the bales when Dad came around the corner of the stack with the tractor and another load of bales.

No matter what I did, where I ran, where I hid, Ted would still find me. He always did.
For the remaining part of the fall I tried to stay away from everyone. I only came into the house when everyone else was in the house and I left the house when everyone left the house. If Mom wanted me to dry the dishes while she went out in the field with everyone, I would quickly get out of the house before Ted came back. I would leave the dishes there undried.

If I was able, I would get Cocoa. If not, I would get on my bike and leave the yard. Sometimes I would hide across the road in the neighbor's bushes and watch the yard. Only when Ted had gone home for the night would I come out of my hiding place and go back to the house. Mom was always mad at me because I never dried the dishes.

I was more terrified of Ted than the coyotes howling behind me in the bush or Mom being mad at me for not doing the dishes.

I could not stay in the house no matter what they said or did to me.

… the death of a spirit ….

I am not sure when I died. I did not remember Nelson being there until many years later, and when I did remember him, it made the memory of my death even worse.

Maybe it was the same year, or maybe it was the following year when I was six when the final brutal attack happened.

Years later, when I asked my parents how long Ted had worked for Dad, and whether it was one or two years or longer, they couldn't remember. It was not a subject that anyone wanted to talk to me about, and trying to get the answers for myself was a touchy subject. I was not sure why. Even thirty years later, after I had finally told my parents about what Ted had done to me, they did not want to deal with it. They did not want to talk to me about it.

For them the memory was better left alone, left where they felt it belonged. Those memories were mine and mine alone; they were not to be talked about.

The final horrific act of abuse happened in the fall. Mom and Dad had gone somewhere and had asked my cousin, Nelson to watch the three of us while they were away for the afternoon.

I will refer to Nelson as my cousin as he is closely related to me.

Nelson was about sixteen and medium height; not really skinny but not heavy either with short brown hair.

My two brothers, Hank and Al and I were playing in the living room when Nelson and Ted came into the house. I was instantly scared, and my mind started to race: *Why is Ted here? Dad is not here, nobody is working today in the field?*

Nelson told Hank and Al to go outside and play, but they did not want to go outside. Ted made sure that they did. I wanted to go outside too, but Nelson stopped me and told me that I was going to stay in the house and play with him and Ted.

I told Nelson that I did not want to play with Ted. I told him that I did not want to stay in the house with them.

Nelson grabbed my arm and told me that I was staying in the house. I tried to pull my arm away. I was almost lying on the floor trying to get away from Nelson's grip when Ted came over and grabbed my other arm.

Ted told me "Today is going to be your special day."

I told him that I did not want it to be my special day. I begged Nelson to tell the Ted to go away, but Nelson said that Ted was staying and that we were all going to play house together.

Nelson said that he wanted to feel special, and that Ted said it was okay if I let him feel special too.
I started to cry and told them that I did not want them to feel special and I did not want to be special. I wanted to go outside with my brothers.

Nelson picked me up by my arms and Ted picked up my legs. I was kicking and crying, trying to get away. As they carried me to the bedroom, Ted was pulling down my panties. He had taken them completely off by the time they got me to the bedroom. Both Nelson and Ted held me down on the bed.

I remember trying to scream, but there was no sound coming out of my mouth. The pain was excruciating and numbing at the same time. I thought and felt that they were killing me.

When they were done raping me, Ted slapped Nelson on the back and said, "Feels real good, hey!"

They both stood there beside the bed looking at me.

I was not moving, not breathing, not living. In my heart I had died.

Nelson said, "What do we do with her?"

Ted said, "Leave her."

Nelson said, "She'll tell."

"No she won't. She hasn't told yet," replied Ted.

Then they both left. I lay there not moving. I did not know how long I lay there. I knew that I had died. My eyes were open but I did not see anything. My heartbeats were really slow and my breathing was shallow. I had no colour in my face or body.
I felt strange. Suddenly I could see myself lying there on the bed, broken and bloody, with creamy white stuff all over the bedspread and me. I was not afraid, I was only sad. I could see a black blanket slowly creeping over me. I could see the emptiness in my soul through my own eyes. All of the beauty and happiness that I had known in my short life was being covered over with the black blanket.

All of the physical pain was gone. I did not hurt anymore. I only felt small and alone. I could see desperation and isolation already starting to grow in my soul. I could feel a suffocating heavy weight on my chest and shoulders.

I am not sure how long I lay there dead. My right arm was lying limp over the side of the bed. I was still on my back with my face facing the closet.
Then, it seemed like there was a grown up woman standing beside the bed looking down at me lying there. She was wearing a long white robe or gown of some sort, and her hair was brown and long

with waves in it. She was so beautiful. She had a white glow around her and her outline was soft and fuzzy looking.

The woman stood there watching me. Then she bent down over the bed beside my dead body and put her hand on my chest. There was a soft white light that radiated into the chest of my little body from her fingers and palm: a warm soft peaceful light.

My body lay there. I could feel something warm on my chest. I did not know what had happened, and I did not know that I was laying on the bed. I was having a hard time breathing. My chest was heavy, like someone had sat on me. My arms and legs would not move very well, it felt like they had gone to sleep. My whole body felt like it had gone to sleep. It was hard to see out of my eyes, but my chest felt very warm.

I could hear someone crying and feel someone pushing at me to get up, but I was not moving. Hank had come back into the house and found me laying on the bed. He grabbed my arm but it fell limp, then he started shaking me and trying to pull me up, but I was just an empty body with no life in it. My eyes continued to stare into space with emptiness in them, they were like two dark brown bottomless pools. There was no depth to them, just emptiness.

Hank was sobbing so hard that he sat down on the floor with his arms wrapped around his knees, slowly rocking himself back and forth. His constant crying finally started to register in my brain. Slowly life started to creep back in to my soul.

Why is it dark outside?
Who is crying?
How come I can't move?
Why is everything fuzzy looking?
Is that my brother sitting there?
I have to help him. Why is he crying, is he hurt?

While Hank was crying I slowly started to come back into my own body. I was groggy and stiff. I pushed myself to sit up. My mind was in a daze as I fixed my dress, found my panties and pulled them on. Then I slid off the side of the bed and sat on the floor beside him. He looked down at me with puffy-red, scared eyes. I told him that everything was going to be okay. We both got up and went outside.

Later that afternoon, after Ted had left, Nelson came back into the house and took the bedspread outside and washed it off. When Mom and Dad came home, Mom noticed the bedspread hanging over the fence outside of the house. She asked Nelson what happened and he told her that I had thrown up on it and he washed it off.

I do not remember seeing Ted after that last attack, and I had no memory of what Nelson had done until many years later. I totally blanked it out from my memory.

I did remember Ted however. I remembered the first attacks but I could not remember the last attack until 40 years later. When I did remember, it felt like all the pieces of the puzzle had finally started to come back, but I was not prepared for when I had fully realized what I had tried to supress so long ago.

At the time after the last brutal attack, I knew that the woman standing there watching me on the bed was an angel.

I felt that the soul of the little girl left that day and another arrived to take its place. I believe that what happened that day with Ted and Nelson was the end of her. They had crushed her soul beyond repair.

The molestation from Ted had been horrible, but the rape was beyond horrible. It killed me.

Sometimes I feel that the soul that I was born with is not the same one that I have today. The first soul was so badly damaged that it could not go on. The brutality and violence from the last attack drove it to seek out a place of peace and love. It could not return back to the body where there was horrible pain, it could not return back to such violence.

Maybe that's a strong reason why I did not lose my mind. Maybe my mind was spared because I was supposed to remember the abuse and the ripple effect it has caused in my life. I was meant to remember so that I could tell this story.

I believe that the first soul stayed connected to the body of the little girl also, but the second soul brought her back to the land of the living and would help in the process of healing. It would be 40 years later when the second helping soul would be released to go back to God's love, its purpose completed.

... possible excuses ...

I have to believe that Nelson wasn't or isn't a bad person. I try to believe that he was under strong influence from Ted, since there were not a lot of teenage boys around where we lived. I tell myself that Nelson had no other boys to hang around with, to talk to about girls, and to do teenage boy things with.

I guess you make friends with who is in your neighbourhood if that is all you have.

I know that these possible excuses, do not make what happened to me right. They do not, in any way, let Nelson off the hook for the part that he played in affecting my life in such a negative way. My parents and I had trusted him to keep me safe.

The abuser, for many people, can be a trusted family member, parent, sibling, step-sibling, adoptive sibling, step-parent, uncle, aunt, cousin or even grandparent. They can also be a person in a position of power and influence: your minister, priest, sports coach, teacher, or counsellor. Unfortunately the list is endless.

However you cut it, Nelson should not have done what he did, and he should not have allowed Ted to get away with it either.

I wonder: how can either one of them live with themselves, knowing what they have done?

Ted was not a normal person, he was sick. I try to believe that Nelson became trapped in Ted's world for a while. Maybe Nelson was lonely and wanted a friend, and maybe he would do anything for that friend to show that he belonged; like rob a bank, or beat up someone. Or maybe he was just as bad as Ted, for who in their right mind would help rape a little girl?

To this day, Nelson has not said that he is sorry for what he did, nor told me why he did it. That tells me that he has no remorse or conscience. That tells me that he is as sick and twisted as Ted, maybe even more so because he is a family member.

Years later, I did confront Nelson and ask him why. His response was "I don't remember anything." Is that convenient, or what? I wish that I could not remember!

After finally remembering Nelson's role in what had happened, I have chosen to keep Nelson at a distance. I don't want him in any part of my life but this has been difficult to say the least, since he will always be a part of my family through blood.

That is the choice that I have made.

... survival ...

After the last attack from Ted and Nelson, both of them disappeared from my conscious life for a long time. I don't believe that Ted ever came back to our house and I think that Nelson went away to a boarding school.

I hope that they both were very worried. I hope that Ted was concerned the Nelson would tell, and that Nelson was afraid that I would tell.

After all, Ted did not have to worry about me telling, he had already taken care of that by terrifying me, but Nelson was another story. Ted would not be able to threaten him to "shut up or I will kill everyone." Nelson was old enough to prevent that from happening. So why did he not tell?

Why did he participate with Ted? And if he knew what Ted had been doing, why did he not stop him from hurting me? Maybe he was afraid of Ted also, but then again maybe not!

I am trying to understand why it happened. I am trying to figure out why Nelson could do such a terrible act. Was Nelson influenced enough by Ted to commit that horrible act, or did Ted have nothing to do with Nelson's decision to sexually attack me?

If you were Nelson, how would you be able to tell the family what you had done to their little girl? How would you be able to live with yourself? How would you be able to look at her knowing what you had done? Would that not eat at your soul?

How was his life changed by that day?

I know how my life was changed. I know that I will never forget or forgive Nelson for what he did.

Nelson will always be in our family. I do not like him, and I may not be able to look at him without disgust. I am not sure that if I even care whether he lives or dies.

I know that I will hate Ted until my dying day. I will never forget or forgive either of them for the effects that they had on my relationship with family and on me. But I do not know if I have the same hatred for Nelson. I guess there are varying degrees of heartbreak, mistrust, and anger.

I feel that I do not need to forgive either one of them in order for me to move on. I have forgiven myself.

Knowing that they both will have to explain themselves one day to a higher power is enough for me. I believe that we will not end up in the same place after this life is over. I don't believe that someone who lives their life trying to help people will go to the same place as someone who tries to destroy lives. Everyone will have their judgement day.

I take a lot of comfort from that fact.

CHAPTER TWO

... the bear ...

I had a hiding spot that was across the road from the yard. From this spot I could see what was going on in the yard, but no one could see me hiding in the thin row of bushes that bordered the hay field behind.

Every time Ted was at our house, I would run and hide there until he left. I would sneak through the trees beside our house and cross the road out of sight of the house. Then I would crawl to the spot where I could see the house and yard. My hiding spot was probably about 50 feet away from our bush line.

Ted arrived in the morning and would leave at night after he had finished helping Dad. I would stay in my hiding spot all day. I never took anything to eat or drink with me. I never knew when Ted would come. I was always afraid he would sneak up on me. I was always looking for him, afraid that he would find me.

Whenever I heard that he was coming or I thought that he was coming I would run and hide there.

I remember the day my hiding spot across the road was not safe anymore.

We had a blind calf born that spring. While the cows and calves were still locked in the corral, the calf was able to locate his mother, but when the cows were turned out into the pasture of new spring grass the calf would lose his mother.

Dad decided that it would probably be best if the calf was tied up at night so it would not get lost or end up as coyote food. When the calf was tied in the trees behind our house, the mother cow would stay close to the pasture fence beside the trees. She was only 10 feet away from her baby.

On each side of our yard was a thick row of trees about 30 feet wide. One side of the house, where our bedrooms were, was about 20 feet from the trees. On the opposite side of the house the trees were probably 500 feet away.

The calf had been tied up in the trees closest to the house and the pasture where his mother was. One morning we went out to let the calf go back to his mother and feed, but when we got there he was gone. We checked the pasture but he was not there. Dad came out to look at the area where the calf had been tied, and he said that a brown or black bear had come in the night and snatched the calf from beside our house.

My mind started to race. A bear had been 20 feet away from me in the night, and a bear had come to put the calf out of his misery. He would no longer be alone at night and afraid without his mother to protect him.

Dad and several of the neighbors decided to go after the bear and shoot it. Dad said that if a bear was not afraid to come into the yard and snatch a calf, it would not be afraid to come in and snatch one of us kids. While they were gone I decided that I needed to find the bear also, maybe it would take me away too. I sneaked into the trees beside the house and started to follow the spotty drag trail of blood from the bear and calf. I went across the road and through the short field into the bush on the other side. My heart was pounding and my hands were shaking. Every few feet I would find blood. But no bear.

Then I could hear Dad shouting and gunfire. The sound of the guns snapped me back to reality. I thought *Oh my God, Dad is going to find me in the bush and be mad at me.* I did not want to make my Dad mad at me, so I gave up my mission to find the bear.

I loved my father very much and would do anything in my power to make him love me. I did not want him to think that I was a bad girl; I did not want him to know that I was a bad girl. After Ted's attacks, he would always say that my Dad would not like me if he knew what I had done.

It was never what Ted had done; it was always what I had done. When you are five you can begin to believe that you are a bad person because of the acts of someone else.

I do not want to be a bad girl. I have to hide the secret from Dad. I can pretend that I am a good girl. Maybe Dad will not know, and maybe Dad will love me. Oh God, I wish the bear had eaten me instead, but I would miss Dad if the bear ate me. I have to get out of the bush before the bear finds me. Run, run as fast as you can, never hide in the bush across from the road, the bear might get me, Dad will never love me. I will die a bad person. They will laugh at me again. Have to work hard at becoming a good girl, have to make my Dad proud of me. But, I can't stay home, Ted will find me.

One more demon to fight. After that I became terrified of bears. This fear has followed me into my adult life, one I have yet to conquer.

... egg shampoo ...

One evening Mom sent me out to the chicken coop to gather eggs. I had been watching a TV commercial about how if you used egg shampoo it would make your hair beautiful and then people would notice how beautiful you looked. The lady on the TV did not look beautiful before she washed her hair with egg shampoo but she looked beautiful after. Everyone noticed her and how beautiful she looked.

I grabbed my pink sand pail and headed toward the chicken coop. It was cool outside, but inside the chicken coop it was warm. I gathered enough eggs to fill my pail, about 12 eggs in all. Instead of heading back to the house, I sat down on the floor of the coop and decided to wash my hair with egg shampoo. I wanted to be beautiful like the lady on TV, then when everyone could see that I was beautiful, they would not be able to see the ugly anymore. I emptied my sand pail, then proceeded to break every egg into it. Then I mixed up all the eggs and put in on my hair and scrubbed my hair like my mom did when she washed it. When I was done, I headed back to the house. By then it was dark outside.

I kept thinking as I headed to the house: *I had better run, the bear might be in the bush ready to grab me.*

When I got back to the house, I stopped on the steps of the porch before going in. I was beautiful, and they would notice that I was beautiful now that I had washed my hair with egg shampoo. I picked the straw out of my dress and then I opened the porch door and went in.

Mom turned to look at me. She just stood there staring at me, then all of a sudden she smiled and asked, "Where are the eggs?" Before I could answer my brothers looked at me and started to laugh, then dad started to laugh. Everyone was laughing at me. I stood there confused and then started to cry. I was totally devastated because the egg shampoo did not work. I was still ugly. I did not know how I was ever going to be able to be beautiful, like the other girls I had seen on TV. Ted had made me ugly and I thought that everyone else saw me as ugly too.

When I think back now, I guess that I did look funny, with my hair sticking out in all directions with slimy egg yolks and whites pasted in it. The air outside was quite cool that night and it had actually stiffened my wet hair. The eggs acted like a stiff mousse.

It took a bit of time to get a dozen eggs out of my hair. This was no small feat for Mom since we did not have running water.

... lonely grade two ...

I entered grade two and during that year had a very hard time focusing on school. I did not have any school friends; I was too afraid someone would see me.

During school I was constantly nervous and fidgeting. When the teacher told me to sit still and behave, that was nearly impossible. So I then started to lick the back of my hands but my legs would continue to bounce up and down. My hands had gotten so chapped that they were red and cracked, and the only way to stop them from itching and hurting was to lick them more. I licked them all the time.

At the end of the school year, I did not know that I had failed. In September when we went back to school, all the kids stood in rows and the teachers called out the names of the kids in their classes. I was horrified to find out that my name was not called to go with my classmates into the new grade three class but had been called to go into grade two again. When I approached the teacher and said that I was in the wrong class, she called the principal over. The principal told me that I would be doing grade two and grade three work, and if I worked hard enough I would be put into grade three after Christmas. I was so embarrassed and felt stupid and ugly.

At recess time, none of the kids in my old grade two class would play with me. They would not even talk to me. None of the new grade two kids would play with me either, they played with their friends from the previous year. Nobody wanted to be my friend. I knew everyone thought I was stupid and they were laughing at me.

Every day I would sit on the bench outside at recess and noon hour all by myself. I was ugly and stupid. In the mudroom kids would make fun of me. No one wanted to be with me.

I could not wait until Christmas, because when I went back to school I would be put into grade three with my friends. But when Christmas break was over and I went back to school I was still in grade two. I was not put in grade three. I was not smart enough to move ahead.

I am ugly and stupid. I don't deserve any friends.
Who'd want to be friends with me?

That was a long and lonely year for me. After that, for the remainder of my school years, I stayed pretty much to myself. I had some friends, but I kept my guard up and never let anyone get too close. I did not want anyone to see that I was ugly on the inside also. Ted had made me ugly.

... the lease, finding my peace ...

All of the horses in my childhood and youth were largely responsible for me keeping my sanity. I would talk to them and tell them all the things that were happening to me with Ted, the other kids in school, the two mean bus drivers and my Mom. The horses never interrupted me or complained about my whining. The horses just listened. They had no judgement.

On one ride when I was 8 or 9, I remember riding out to the leased land where our cattle were pasturing for the summer. This was my favorite place, as it was located way out in the bush, away from everybody and about three miles from our house across the river. Cocoa and I walked along the windy trail with its up and down hills, across the little creek and around the bend to the barbed-wire gate at the entrance into the pasture. I slid off to open the gate, led Cocoa through, and then closed the gate again. To the right side of us was the start of Horseshoe Lake (I thought it was a lake but it was really a big slough). On the left side, through the trees and down a steep embankment, was the river and straight ahead was the cattle trail. I jumped up on Cocoa and headed straight down the cattle trail for some time, until I came to the fork in the trail. I could either go left further along the river and back into one of the other open pasture areas or head to the right and follow the lake. I headed right.

It was a gorgeous day, the sun was high in the sky, the Indian paintbrushes were blooming and wild tiger lilies and bluebells were scattered amongst the trees. As Cocoa and I continued walking on the trail, we soon came to the first big pasture. There were a few cows munching grass around the old corrals, but nothing else. Cocoa and I headed over to the bank of the lake. I slid off, tied her to the tree, patted her and walked over to the edge of the water and sat down.

There was a stillness there, and the air was calm. I sat there and breathed in the heavenly scent of the flowers, dried cow manure and the water. I watched the ducks bobbing for food and beavers swimming across the water dragging trees to their dens. The cows had eaten down all of the grass, so I could see and hear all the noises coming from the lake. As I sat there basking in the rays from the sun, I suddenly heard crashing coming from across the lake.

The lake was maybe an eighth of a mile wide and shaped like a horseshoe. I would estimate that it was maybe a mile long.

I was not afraid. I sat there not moving, waiting to see what was going to come out of the bush. Soon more crashing came from the bush. This time the sound was a little closer. I waited, watching the other side of the lake.

There was no shore, the trees had grown right up to the edge of the water, and so whatever was making the noise was going to be walking into the water soon.

As I watched and listened, I started to daydream. As the sun was warming on my face and my body was starting to relax, I started drifting away. My shoulders were slumping a bit and my stomach muscles were also relaxing. My head was getting heavy, and I laid back and closed my eyes.

I not sure how long I slept but when I woke up the cows were all around me, sniffing my head and body. As I slowly sat up I shooed them away with my hand and noticed, standing directly opposite me on the other side of the lake was a cow moose and calf. They were standing in the water eating the vegetation that was growing on the lakeshore.

The sun was starting to go down behind the trees. It was time to start home before it became too dark in the bush.

These peaceful interludes were the only thing that I could count on. They were the only time that I could relax and breathe without fear of someone finding me and hurting me again.

... our neighbours ...

As time went on, soon other families started to buy land to start their own dream for a farm. The couple that bought land behind our property, the Jensen's, were friends of Mom's and Dad's from Southern Alberta.

The Jensen's had two girls, Anna and Leigh, that were about four and six years younger than me. I was about ten when I started to go to their house to spend the day playing. They lived mile and a half away. Sometimes I would walk, but most times I would ride Cocoa across the neighbor's field to their house.

In the next year or two, Mrs. Jensen would ask me to watch the girls if she had to run to town for groceries.

It was a hot summer day. Their mom asked me to watch the two girls while she ran to town. Soon I became bored with just playing in their front yard, which was considerably smaller than our yard by a third, so I asked the girls if they wanted to ride Cocoa down to their dad's lease where he kept his cattle for the summer. Cocoa was in the small corral at the back of their yard eating hay. I always put her there when I visited them.

Their lease was directly north of their property and bordered the river but on the opposite side of my dad's lease. It also was mostly bush with small pastures located all around it.

I caught Cocoa and put on her bridle. The three of us climbed on and headed off down to their field, about a mile and a half, then turned left into the bush toward the gate for the lease.

Cocoa was pretty relaxed about having lots of kids on her. Once I jumped on Cocoa then I would bend down over her left side, stiffen my foot, and then grab Anna's hand and start to pull her up. Once she was high enough to step on my foot, which I held out stiff and straight for her, she could swing over her leg over Cocoa's back and I could grab her shorts and pull her onto the horse. I repeated this with Leigh. Soon I was in front, with Anna hanging on behind me and Leigh hanging onto Anna.

I had to get off to open the gate, then lead Cocoa through. Then I closed the gate. I pulled both the girls off, so that I could jump back on Cocoa, then helped them back on. When we were all on Cocoa, then we followed the cattle trail down the steep hill into the first pasture. Cocoa had to go very slowly as the hill was very steep. I had to hold onto Cocoa's mane and push myself backward because Anna and Leigh were sliding forward as we descended down the hill. Once at the bottom, everyone squirmed back into place on Cocoa's back and we continued on.

It was so quiet and calm down on the bottom part of the lease. We rode for a while, enjoying the hot sun on our backs, looking at all the berries and flowers, and smelling the heavenly-rich aroma of Saskatoon berries and wild raspberries.

Before long we arrived at the river, and the mouth of Sturgeon Creek that flowed into the Little Smoky River. We all slid off. I tied Cocoa to a tree and we headed for the water. There was a three foot bank that we had to slide down to get to the sand bar on the river.

The sun had heated up the sand to so much that it was painful to step on it with our bare feet, so we were forced to sit down in the sand.

Sitting there was peaceful, and I ran my hands through the sand, feeling the small grains flow through my fingers. Before long, the river started to call our names. It looked so inviting, so cool. We did not bring our bathing suits, but that did not matter, we stripped off our shirts and shorts and ran, yipping and howling from the hot sand to the river in our underwear. It felt great to step into the warm water. Anna and Leigh promptly sat down at the edge with the water lapping around their bottoms. I told the girls to stay on the edge of the river, while I went to find a long stick to check for holes under the water.

I remember that several people had drowned in this river from falling into sink holes that were under the water. I believed that if I used the stick and walked into the water poking the stick into the bottom of the river, I would detect a sink hole before anyone stepped in it and drowned. So with caution and excitement I staked out a swimming area for us to swim in. The area was about 20 feet wide and 30 feet long, and the water was up to my thighs. The current was too strong if I went further into the river.

While I was doing this, Anna and Leigh stayed near the shore. They did not know how to swim if they fell into a sink hole. I wouldn't be able to save them, because I did not know how to swim either.

In my mind it was okay if I fell into the hole. No one was going to miss me. But Anna's and Leigh's parents would miss them. They were very concerned about them all the time, hollering for them when we were outside playing, always wanting to know where they were. The constant checking where we were at was frustrating to me. Mom never hollered for me, ever. I couldn't understand why their mom and dad did.

We played there for hours swimming by crawling on our hands and kicking our legs. We made sand castles and pretended that we were wild horses galloping on our hands and knees through the water.

It was a great day, one on my best days. There was no fear, not even of the cougars and bears in the area.

... Sailor ...

Dad had helped out a friend and bought his stallion named "Sailor." Sailor was a dark bay with a white star and stripe down his nose. His mane and tail were black and the bottom parts of his legs where white.

When Sailor came to our place, he started to chase and tried to mount Cocoa all of the time. This behaviour went on for several months. One day when I was out riding Cocoa her hind legs went out from under her. I ran and told Dad that there was something the matter with Cocoa's back legs. Dad checked over her hind legs, then he got really was angry and said that the stallion had crippled Cocoa's hindquarters. So with the help of three other guys, Dad gelded him.

I used to always feed Sailor fresh rhubarb from the garden. When he ate it he would curl up his top lip and flop it around. It looked funny; Sailor always made me laugh. Dad always told me to be careful around him. I guess he thought that Sailor might hurt me, but I knew that he would not. One day I forgot my blue wool coat that Mom had knitted for me, at the corral. Sailor found my coat first, and he decided to play with it and chew it up. When I finally found my coat it was lying in the corral, or should I say "the remnants of my coat" Were there. I was sure mad at him for that.

I loved that coat, it was a medium blue color with two rearing horses on the front and a big white rearing horse on the back. I begged Mom to make me another one, but she never did.

Dad later sold Sailor after he tried to hurt Nelson. Sailor was being ridden by Nelson in the ditch when Sailor reared up and fell over on top of Nelson, nearly killing him. I don't remember the accident, but I do remember being sad because Sailor was going to be sold. I was so angry the day Sailor left, I kept thinking it was all Nelson's fault. He was stupid and could not ride. He always thought that he was a shit-hot horse person. I thought he was just stupid, and now Sailor was gone.

In my heart I knew that I would have been able to ride Sailor. I knew that Sailor would not hurt me. But nobody would let me ride him.

Cocoa was getting old and her hind legs were very arthritic so I was unable to ride her anymore. I was looking forward to buying a new horse. It would be a good distraction from my fears and worries.

... a baby?????...

For years, I used to wonder how I was going to tell Mom and Dad that I was going to have a baby. For nine long years I fretted about it.

This fretting affected many aspects of my young life. I was always afraid someone would be able to tell what had happened.

I was afraid there was something strange about me that made people want to do bad things to me. I did not know that what they did to me was not normal; I only knew that I did not like it and did not want it to happen again. But I was afraid that there was something about me that made people want to hurt me. I was so scared that it would happen again.

Have to run, have to hide, so alone, so scared.
Ted always told me that I had wanted it. Did he mean that I wanted him to do it to me? Did I make him do it to me? If I made him do it, how could I make him stop? How can I change what it is about me that made him do it?

I didn't know what to change. I was so afraid that someone else would see what Ted saw and want to do it to me too. I didn't want anyone else to do it. I was so scared.

I have to run, have to hide, can't let anyone see me,
can't let anyone see what Ted saw.
But what did he see? I look normal in the mirror,
what do they see?
I'm so scared, so alone, have to run, have to hide.

... 1969 ...

It was a typical hot summer afternoon. Mom wanted me to babysit my little sister Dottie again. She always wanted me to babysit. Dottie was two years old and I was twelve.

I felt that Dottie was Mom's kid, not mine. Why should I always have to look after her? I had to look after myself. I had to protect myself, and I could not do that if I had to protect Dottie too. I felt that Mom should look after Dottie herself, or find someone else that could look after her and protect her.

I told Mom that I did not want to babysit Dottie and I ran outside and hid on the floorboard of Dad's blue pickup truck that was parked by the back door of the house. I knew that I needed to be able to escape from Ted. I lay on the floor under the steering wheel in a fetal position, scared. Terrified that Ted would find me in the house, scared that he would find Dottie too.

My mind was racing: *Scared, have to hide!*

The driver's door window in the truck was down. Mom came bursting out of the back door of the house looking for me. Dad came up to the house and asked Mom, "What are you mad about. Mom replied, "I want to put Brenda in a foster home because I don't know how to handle her. Mom said, "Brenda is lazy and will not help me around the house. She will not do the dishes or babysit Dottie." Then Mom said to Dad, "I am afraid that she would hurt Dottie because she is jealous of her.

Dad replied, "We're not going to send Brenda away."

Then I heard the door open and close. Both Mom and Dad went into the house to continue their conversation about sending me away or not sending me away. I hoped that Dad would win, but I was not sure if he would. I guessed that I would have to wait and see.

I laid on the floor of the truck for hours, hiding and crying. I hated Mom. I knew that she had never liked me. She was always trying to get me to stay at home. I could not stay at home. I had to be able to escape. I could not stay where someone could find me, could corner me.

They did not understand, they did not care.

Mom and Dad never knew that I had overheard what they had said. Mom never knew that I had heard with my own ears that she did not want me; that she wanted to give me away.

She had her perfect little girl, Dottie.

I thought to myself: *Why would she want me? Why would anyone want me? Dad wants me though, he said "No" to Mom.*

I think that was one of the most devastating days of my life, realizing that my own mother did not want me. Our relationship from that point forward was very turbulent. We fought constantly and one time had a very physical fight.

Because I refused to stay at home for any length of time, Mom soon started to call me "The Roadrunner" and it was not meant in a kind way. Mom and I were strangers living in the same house. Sadly we remained that way until she died.

Trying to put my past behind me has been a challenge to say the least, but I have survived, and will continue to survive the events of my childhood. I did not ask Ted or Nelson to abuse me. I did not deserve it.

What I did deserve was for the members of my family that I had trusted and the people that my parents trusted to respect that trust, and not to use it for their own personal gain and enjoyment.

If they thought for one minute that I would not remember what they did to me, both of them were sadly mistaken. Their secrets are not safe with me anymore, for I have found my voice.

... Father Gender, the priest ...

From the time I was ten to my early teenage years, the local priest named Father Gender would arrive at our house every Sunday around noon for lunch after his morning service in our town. He was on his way to the next town to deliver his Sunday afternoon service.

Father Gender was a kindly elderly man with graying hair. On his round face he wore small round glasses and he had a warm smile. He was not very tall, and had a portly belly. He always wore his black wide-brimmed hat and a black coat.

When he arrived, we all would sit around the table eating lunch with him. He never preached to my parents about not going to church. Instead he talked about farming with Dad, the economy or whatever else happened to be the topic of the day.

It did not matter to Father Gender that we were not catholic. I believe that he found us to be a good Christian family that had values despite not going to church. To me, Father Gender was what a true Christian was. It did not matter what colour you were, or whether you were rich or poor, as long as you lived your life according to the Ten Commandments.

Father Gender had met my Dad when Dad was doing carpenter work on the Catholic church and the nuns' residence. While Dad was working there, Father Gender and the nuns would make Dad lunch and they would talk about life. Sometimes I would go with Dad to the church and play in the pews while he worked there.

Father Gender gave me my faith in God, not by preaching it to me, but by his kindness towards me. I believe that he could see my soul, and knew what it really was like. He gave me hope where there was none.

CHAPTER THREE

... hitchhiking ...

It was a beautiful summer day. I was at home alone babysitting Dottie. I was thirteen, and she was three. Mom and Dad were up at the local Auction Market at the cattle sale. I had wanted to go, but Mom said that I had to stay at home with Dottie.

Staying at home drove me crazy, so I decided to take Dottie and walk to town, about 7 miles. I never phoned Mom to tell her that we were coming because I knew she would have told me that I had to stay at home with Dottie.

It would be a surprise, probably not a pleasant one, but I didn't care. I didn't want to be home alone and not be able to run and get away. Babysitting Dottie was like a heavy weight on my shoulders. How could I protect her if I would not be able to protect myself?

I knew that I would not get a spanking because my parents would both be too busy at the sale.

Dottie and I had walked about ½ mile from home when a car stopped and the driver offered to pick us up. He was a young man, clean shaven with nice clothes, in his early twenties, I had never seen him before or seen his car on the road before. I would have remembered that car. It was light blue with leather seats, the car was so clean on the inside, like brand new.

The window was already down on the passenger side of the car, and the guy leaned over and said that it was raining across the river and that he would give us a ride to town. Before getting into the car I looked behind me down the road towards the river but I could not see any rain.

I thought that if the man was going to do anything to me, it probably would not matter because nobody cared anyway. I knew that Dottie would be safe because nobody ever hurt her. She did not have the look, only I had the look.

For as much as I felt trapped in the chore of babysitting Dottie, I was also very protective of her. I did not want what happened to me to happen to her, and that was a huge burden. I became a buffer of sorts, I thought that if anyone was looking at her that way, I would shield her with my body, they could have my body instead of hers. After all I already was ugly.

We got into the front seat of the car; Dottie sat on my lap. He asked where we were going and I told him that we were going to the Auction Market. The man said that he would drop us off the motel close to the Auction Market and we could walk to rest of the way.

When we arrived at the Auction Market I went to find Mom to let her know that we were there. She was not impressed to see me, but what could she do? She could not send us back home and everyone was too busy to drive us.

Dottie and I stayed at the Auction Market until the sale was finished, then we all went home.

I am not sure why, but I never did hitchhike again after that. I also do not remember babysitting Dottie again during an auction sale.

... I am leaving ...

Mom and I were always fighting. We had just had another fight about me not doing the dishes and not helping out around the house. She said, "Why are you always so lazy?"

So I turned my head to glare at her and said, "I am not lazy! I hate doing the stupid dishes, why do I always have to do the dishes, why can't the boys do the dishes?"

I would rather have worked outside in the field picking roots and rocks than be in the house doing stupid dishes. At least out in the field I could see if anyone was coming and run, but in the house I had nowhere to go. I was trapped.

Mom said: "You are useless! I am going to tell your dad. He'll straighten you out and you'll be sorry!"

I hated her. She was always trying to turn Dad against me.

I told her that I was running away and that she would never see me again. Mom just ignored me.

When I got outside the boys were laughing at me and said: "Good riddance to bad rubbish."

Every time I was in trouble, Al and Hank would stand outside on the steps and listen at the door to the fight. I know that they hoped that I would get a spanking from Dad. I hated them for that. They always wanted me to get a spanking.

After leaving the house, I started to walk down the driveway. When I got to the end, I looked back. No one was looking for me, nobody cared if I left. I slowly started to walk down the gravel road. When I reached the end of our land, about ½ mile, I looked back to see if anyone was coming to get me, but there was no one coming. I hoped that someone would come, that someone cared that I was running away.

It was another hot summer day, the air was still around me, and it seemed like everything had deserted me. There were no birds flying in the sky, no bugs biting, just me, all alone, so I continued walking. Every once in a while I would look back toward our driveway in the hopes that someone was coming, hoping to see if Mom was coming to get me.

If only Mom would come; she knows that I'm running away, why won't she come?
She won't come because she doesn't want me, she is glad that I am gone.
Nobody wants me!

It took a couple of hours for me to reach the house near the top of the hill, which was about two miles from our house. There were kids outside playing on a swing set and I hoped that they would ask me to join them. I didn't want to be alone. I hoped that someone would want me. So when I reached their driveway, I stopped and yelled "Hi" to them.

The two girls on the swing looked at me and told me to shut up. I continued walking.

I could hear them laughing at me. I felt so alone, I felt so angry. I hated those girls, I hated Mom. I hated everyone. I wished that those two girls would fall off their swing and die!

When I reached the very top of the hill, I had two choices. If I continued to walk over the crest of the hill I would not be able to see if anyone was coming for me, and if I stopped and sat down on the side of the road I would be able to see if anyone drove out of our driveway. If anyone came for me I would have enough time to run into the bush beside the road and hide.

It'll serve them right if they can't find me.
They'll be worried and they'll start yelling for me.
They'll be sorry that I'm gone.

I sat down and waited, and waited, and waited. Several hours passed. It was going to get dark soon. Still no one came for me.

While I waited I tossed pebbles into the bush. Several cars went by, but no one stopped to ask me why I was there. I was invisible.

I soon realized that nobody was coming for me. I felt so defeated, even when I told them I was leaving they did not care.
I got up and started to walk back home.

… the leather strap …

A few days later, Mom and I had another fight. This time Dad was in the house. Mom told Dad that she didn't know what to do with me and that he had better straighten me out. I am not sure what she was complaining about, as I was doing the dishes after all.

Dad got up from the chair and stomped over to the drawer that held the leather straps.

The leather straps were 12 inches long and 2 inches wide with white thread knots on the underside. They were pieces from an old horse harness; the stitching had broken on the underside and formed little knots. They smarted when you were hit with them. It did not take much effort to cause a lot of pain.

I was standing beside the sink drying Mom's stupid dishes when Dad came up behind me. I turned around to face him. I told him that I would be good and dry the dishes.

His lips were pressed tightly together. He said "That's not good enough!"

He hit me on the leg with the strap. I grabbed my leg with my hand, he hit me again on the same leg, this time also hitting the back of my hand. My hand started to burn and a welt formed immediately.

Dad continued to hit me over and over again. I yelled at him to stop, but he wouldn't. I was backed into the corner of the cupboards. I could not get away. My legs were stinging, but he continued hitting me. I could feel my legs shaking and then they buckled and I fell to the floor. I lay on the floor beside the garbage can in a fetal position, crying, begging for Dad to quit, but he did not listen. He just kept hitting me.

My whole body ached. I could not move. I could only sob. It was hard to breathe. My chest was tight, and my back, legs and arms were all stinging from the hits. I had welts all over my body. My voice was hoarse. I could barely whisper as I pleaded; "Please quit hitting me."

Laying there on the floor beside the garbage I thought, *How fitting to be lying with the rest of the trash.*

I wanted to die. I hoped to die. I did not want to live at home anymore, but I had no place to go. Nobody wanted me. I was trapped.

Dad stood over me shaking the strap at me, yelling at me to smarten up and to help Mom around the house. As I lay there on the floor, I could hear the boys outside laughing. Mom was standing behind Dad with a smirk on her face. When Dad moved away, I slowly got up off the floor. It hurt to move but I refused to cry any more. I struggled to catch my breath, but every time I breathed in it would sound like a sob. I was determined not to give any of them the satisfaction of seeing me cry. I tried not to breath very much, instead I focused on taking in slow shallow breaths. I was not going to let them see me sob.

I walked back over to the sink with my tea towel and continued to dry the dishes. I stood there like a rock, refusing to look at Mom, refusing to acknowledge that she was standing there.

When I was finished the dishes, with my back to her, I asked if I could go outside. She said "Fine." I went down the five stairs on to the porch. My legs were still shaking as well as my hands. I opened the door and there stood Al and Hank. They started to laugh at me and mimicked what I sounded like while Dad was beating me. I refused to say anything to them. My body was trembling, my hands were shaking. It was hard to walk. I had to hang on; I did not want to fall down again. I did not want them to see me crushed. I straightened my back bone, clenched my jaw, and stomped away.

I headed out to the corral. I wanted to find my horse. I wanted to run away. I wanted to hide.

At that moment I told myself, *They'll never see me cry again, ever!*

When I reached the corral, I leaned against the fence. My body was still shaking and my legs were weak. It had taken all my strength just to make it that far. I found Cocoa standing in the corner of the cattle shed, resting in the shade that the shelter provided from the hot sun. I did not have the strength to jump on her so I just stood there her hugging her and sobbing into her long mane.

I was getting angry as I stood there crying in Cocoa's mane. I was getting confused about my feelings for my dad. I thought that he liked me but then I started to think about why my dad did it.

I don't know if I can ever forgive you Dad for betraying me.
You chose Mom's side, you believed what she said about me.
Why can you not see me for who I am?
Instead you see me through Mom's eyes like everyone else in the family does.

To me, everybody in the family treated me the same way Mom did. By example she had taught them not to see me as a person but as a disappointment to the family.

For over twenty years, Dad would brag to my friends about how he had to give me "a licking" and how he smartened me up. Over the years, each time he told the story my age would be older. Soon I was sixteen when I got the beating, not 12 or 13.

When I was first engaged to Alfred, Dad especially enjoyed telling the story.

The last time Dad told the story was at Christmas time 2000. My daughter and her fiancé were spending Christmas day with us. I was joking around with my daughter and she was getting smart with me. Everyone was laughing. Dad jokingly said to my daughter that she was not too big to give a spanking to. That prompted him to tell his favorite story about me.

When he was finished the story, he proceeded to say that I still was not too old for another "spanking." I interrupted him and said that he did not give me a spanking when I was sixteen, he had given me a beating when I was 12. I told him that he should not be proud of the fact that he had beaten me.

I was humiliated and embarrassed sitting there with my daughter and her future husband. I thought, *What a stupid way to be remembered: here sits the woman that was given a beating by her Dad when she was 13, because she was lazy.*

Nobody understood that I did not just dislike dishes. I hated dishes! I knew that I needed to avoid dishes at all costs.

I was happy enough to work outside where I could escape.

In my subconscious mind I was terrified that I would become trapped again by Ted and thanks to my cousin, I was also afraid of members of my family.

The decisions that my subconscious mind made pertaining to the abuse were profound.

I did not understand at that age what was happening to me; why I was always afraid; why I avoided the house when no one else was home. I never would go into the house by myself. If I needed a drink of water, I drank from the barrel outside or the cattle's water tank. If I was hungry I grabbed carrots from the garden and if I needed to go to the washroom, I went in the bush.

When I was forced to be in the house doing housework, while everyone else was outside, I would almost go crazy. I was edgy and panicky. If my fear got the better of me, I would simply leave the dishes in the sink to dry on their own and run away until everyone came home.

They did not understand. They did not try.

... my saviours ...
1970

Twice a year, there was a horse auction in town. Horses were brought from all over the Peace Country to the sale to be sold. There were buyers that traveled around the country purchasing horses from people that could not get their horses to the Auction Market. Dad knew these men and trusted their judgement regarding the horses that they brought to the sale.

Going to the horse auction was my dream every year, and there was nothing that could stop me from going.

Dad had promised me that I could buy one of the horses that the buyers had brought in for the sale. He made a deal with the buyer that I would pay $100.00 for the horse of my choice, and all that I had to do was to go into the back of the Auction Market to the holding pens of these horses and pick one out. Then I was to find Dad and tell him the number that was stuck on the horse's back for identification.

Finally the sale day arrived and I was thrilled to get there. After arriving, I headed straight to the back of the Auction market where the horses were held in the special pens for me. There were horses everywhere, big ones, small ones, horses of every colour. The smell was heavenly. I slowly walked to the four pens that held the horses. In each pen there were approximately 25 horses milling about. I climbed up on the gate and stood there looking for the perfect horse, the one horse that I would get to ride home.

There! Right there, she's the one I want, the little appaloosa mare.
I was so excited. I had always wanted an appaloosa.

I had read about appaloosas and dreamed about them. I thought
that they were the most beautiful horses. They looked so exotic, so
wild and free. I used to pretend I was an appaloosa running free. I
would gallop across the lawn on my hands and knees, fleeing from
dangers, running wild.

I wrecked many pairs of pants with green grass stains on the knees.
The tops of my bare feet, the palms of my hands and my knees
always had green stains on them.

I jumped off the gate surging with excitement. I ran to find Dad
and tell him that I had found the horse I was going to buy.

Sale time was getting close, and the stands were filling up with
people either selling a horse or buying one. The meat buyers had
arrived, and were sitting scattered in the first two rows of the seats.
I hated the meat buyers, I did not know how someone could buy a
horse and know it was going to die.

I climbed to the top of the stands so that Dad could see and waited
in anticipation for my new horse to go through the ring.

The tack was sold first. There were saddles, blankets, bridles,
halters, lead ropes, brushes, saddle pads, everything that you could
think of for your horse. I did not need any of it. I only rode my
horse with a bridle, and that was sitting in the car waiting for me to
grab it.

I sat there anxious, fidgeting, thinking *Oh please hurry, bring out
the horses, bring out my new horse.*

Finally the tack sale was finished and soon the horses would be
brought in to sell. The Auction Market workers brought in
wheelbarrow loads of shavings and spread them around on the
cement floors so that the horses would not slip when brought into
the ring for everyone to see and bid on. After that was finished

then the horses started to sell. I waited as several horses were sold, watching each horse that came into the ring intently. Some were ridden, some were chased, some had sores on their legs from accidents before arriving at the sale, and some were babies.

There she is, she's coming through the door, #58, there's my horse! Dad was in the auctioneer's box, he worked there during the sale. He started to talk about her. He said that she is P.O.A. (Pony of America) and was 7 years old, broken to ride. Then they started to get ready to auction her off to the highest bidder.

The auctioneer asked if anyone would give him $500.00, then $400, then $300, then $200. I waited until he asked for $100 dollars and quickly put my hand up along with several other bidders. The price quickly climbed back to $500. I kept bidding every time someone outbid my last offer. I was so excited that I could hardly sit, but I had to be cool. No one was supposed to know that you were bidding or else they would bid against you. I had to be cool. I liked the vantage point from the top seat, I could see the other bidders, but they could not see me bidding. I watched for the slight nod of the head, the flick of the bidding card or an ever so slight finger wave to show the auctioneer they were bidding. Once the auctioneer knew that you were bidding then you could become very subtle. The auctioneer knew most of the people that were always bidding, the meat buyers.

Finally the hammer fell and my horse was sold to bidder number 3 for $500.00.

Wow, that was me. I had just bought my first horse! I raced down the steps and around the corner of the stands, out the front door of the market and to the car to get my bridle. Then I ran back to the office to pay for my horse. I had to wait for a bit because the sale slips from the sold horses had not arrived in the office yet. When the slips finally arrived I paid my $100 dollars and raced to the back to the pens to see my horse.

... Dragon Seed ...

There she was standing in a pen all by herself, I climbed over the fence and walked over to her. She sure was small, Cocoa was bigger than her. But oh, her hair was so soft!
She was grey with small black spots all over her body. Her eyes were the softest brown with gold flecks in them. I had never seen such gorgeous eyes with pale pink eyelids before, then I noticed that her muzzle was also pink. I looked at her hooves to see if they had the Appaloosa black and cream colored stripes that ran down from the coronet band to the bottom of the hoof, and they did.

I thought that she was the most beautiful colored horse I had ever seen and she was mine. Her breed was called Pony of America, P.O.A. for short. And I was going to name her "Dragon Seed," for her awesome coloring

I put on her bridle and jumped on. It was not far to jump on her since I was used to jumping on Cocoa, but I had to be careful that I did not over jump and fall off the other side. I petted her and showed her off to anyone who cared to look at her. One of the workers came over and said that she looked pretty nice. I was beaming.

After the sale was over I led Dragon Seed out through the back pens, jumped on and headed for home. It was a peaceful ride. We went through the back part of town and along several gravel roads going cross-country. Once we were away from town and the vehicles I could let her trot or gallop without worrying that she would spook at the vehicles. Dragon Seed and I had a lot to talk about. I told her that she and Shep and I were going to have fun and go on lots of adventures together.

Shep was my dog, I had gotten him as a puppy from the Clarks, friends of Mom's and Dad's. He was a golden color with hazel eyes, and my protector. Whenever I went riding or biking, Shep came along.

With my horse and dog as protectors I never had to worry about getting hurt. When Shep was with me I was not afraid of Ted or anyone else. I knew that Shep would get them, he would tear them to shreds.

I soon found out that Dragon Seed had a stubborn streak and would not leave our yard. She quickly became herd bound to Cocoa. I had a battle with her every time I wanted to go for a ride.

One day I was supposed to go riding with a couple of older girls, Shelby and Yvette. Yvette lived across the river about 10 miles away. The three of us were heading to her house for the day. The girls arrived in our yard with their big bay horses. Dragon Seed was having one of her tantrums. I could not get her to go past the house, every time I would be almost past she would spin around and try to run back to the corral where Cocoa was whinnying.

Dad had been watching the problem I was having from the dining room window. He came out of the house, walked over to the garage and brought out his saddle. He walked over to us and told me to get off. Then Dad put the saddle on Dragon Seed. She was not impressed, but Dad got on her.

It looked rather funny because Dad's feet were only about 12 inches off the ground. Dad cranked Dragon Seed's head to the side with the reins and kicked her in the ribs, forcing her to spin in a tight circle. This went on for quite a while until finally Dad got her past the house, but the fun was only beginning. Dragon Seed started to buck. She bucked across the front yard in front of the house, she bucked in and out of the bush on the east side of the house. She was trying to rub Dad off her back in the trees. Dad kept kicking her and she kept bucking.

I felt sick to my stomach. I prayed for her to stop bucking. I did not want her hurt.

Dragon Seed was on a mission and no amount of praying from me was going to stop her. She had to come to terms with the fact that

Dad was not going to go anywhere, and that she had to behave and do what she was told to do.

Finally she quit bucking. Dad rode her over to me and got off. He was covered in sweat. He handed me the reins, and told me to ride her with the saddle on and to make her listen to me.
I got on her and rode out of the yard with the other two girls. Dragon Seed was puffing, her nostrils were flaring, and she was soaked from tips of her ears to the bottom of her butt, but she never pulled the spinning stunt again.

The following spring I had to sell Dragon Seed in the next horse auction. The money I got from her could go towards a better horse my dad said.

Again I could pick out any horse that I wanted for $100.00.

... Buster ...

Buster was a brown and white pinto gelding, he had one blue eye and one brown eye. His mane was white with black streaks and his tail was all black. He was bigger than Cocoa. It was easier getting on him because I did not have to worry about landing on the ground on the opposite side like I did with Dragon Seed.

Buster and I got along fine. He was easy to catch, which was great because Cocoa at times was not when I used to ride her. I would set up two square straw bales in a straight line in the field and jump over them with Buster. He was not afraid of anything and neither was I when I was on his back.

It was early summer and time to chase the cows down to the lease land that was across the river. The lease was where Dad's cattle spent the summer and early fall feeding on the luscious grass. In the fall they came home for the winter where Dad had all the hay stacked in stacks for winter feeding. Every week, Dad would go to the lease to check on the cows and calves to make sure that they were okay. He would check for injuries from the roots and stumps, if any were stuck in the muskeg and if a bear or cougar had killed one of them. Since the lease bordered the river there were always bears, cougars and even lynxes around the cattle as well as non-carnivorous animals such as elk, moose and deer.

Dad had decided that Al should ride Buster instead of running on foot behind the cows all the way to the lease. Buster, however, had other ideas about Al riding him.

Dad saddled up Buster for Al. I stood there mad as hell that Al was going to ride my horse. Al thought it was funny and kept smirking at me. I protested to Dad that I did not want anyone riding my horse, but my protests fell on deaf ears.

Al rode Buster out to the corrals on the other side of the bushes on the east side of the yard. He started to kick Buster to get him to go faster. I yelled at him to quit kicking my horse. Al turned his head around to grin at me, then kicked Buster again in the ribs with his boots. Buster promptly bucked once, unseating Al and connected with Al's knee with his hind hoof as he fell off. Al lay there on the ground crying. Buster galloped over to me. I patted him and calmed my horse down. I did not care that Al had gotten bucked off. I thought that he should not have been riding my horse in the first place and he deserved it for kicking my horse.

Dad, on the other hand, was not sympathetic to Buster and stomped over to him and grabbed the reins. He swung himself up into the saddle and kicked Buster in the ribs hard. Away they went bucking around the pasture. This went on for some time, as people driving by started to stop on the side of the road to watch the rodeo between Dad and Buster. Buster was grunting and bucking while Dad was swearing and kicking. I stood there horrified at the scene that was playing out before my eyes. A large knot was in the pit of my stomach and tears rolled down my face. I was afraid that Buster was going to get hurt.

When Buster finally quit bucking, there were 15 cars parked along the road honking their horns and cheering for Dad. Dad rode Buster over to Al and got off. He handed Al the reins, but Al told Dad that he preferred to run behind the cattle and that he did not want to ride Buster. Al glared at me and said "give Brenda back her stupid horse."

I quickly ran over and took the reins from Dad before he could say anything. Buster was soaking wet. I took the saddle off, dumping it on the ground and jumped on him bareback. Buster and I helped chase the cattle to the lease that day.

Over the winter Buster and Cocoa were put in the corrals with the cows. The cows started to calve in February, but there was a problem. The boys told Dad that Buster was chasing the new calves and biting them.

Buster had to be sold in April at the next horse sale.

I was heartbroken. Again I was told that I could take the money from Buster and buy a new horse for $100.00.

... Volcano ...

I stood on the gate at the Auction Market looking at the horses in the pen. I could see a big bay mare standing there all alone away from the other horses. I could not see her number on her hip, part of it was ripped off. I figured that I would be able to recognize her anyway when she came through the ring.

After I purchased her, I went to the back to see her. I stood there looking at her with wonder. Did I just buy her? Did I buy the wrong horse?

She had big feet with small feathers (long hair hanging off the back of the lower legs and fetlocks), and her head was huge and her withers were monstrous. She was probably the ugliest horse I had ever seen. Suddenly I felt sorry for her.

How could I think she was ugly? I knew what it felt like to be ugly and not wanted. I walked over to her, patted her neck and told her that I was going to take care of her and love her.

I put on her bridle and jumped on. I just sat up there looking at the length of her back before nudging her forward. Her back seemed to go on forever. She had the longest back I had ever sat on. I was positive you could seat three people on her back easily.

I promptly called her "Volcano": large and powerful.

It was autumn, and time to bring the cattle home from the lease. Mom was riding my older brothers' Arabian gelding, a friend from school named Edna, was riding the other Arabian mare, and Dad was riding his saddle horse "Lady," a quarter horse mare. I was riding Volcano.

As we approached the river, the other horses refused to cross the bridge. Dad asked me if I could get Volcano to go across first. I knew Volcano would cross the bridge since I had already been riding her to the lease all summer.

Volcano would go through anything and across anything.

Volcano obliged and walked across the bridge, and the rest of the horses followed her. I was so proud of her, she was brave and fearless, and so was I when I was riding her. Throughout the day when we encountered deep ditches or beaver dams the other horses refused to cross them. Volcano and I would ride out in front of the other horses and cross first, then the other horses would follow her.

Sometimes it was scary crossing the beaver dams because the trail was only wide enough for the horses' feet with a steep drop off one side of the path. The drop off was a wall full of twigs and branches that the beavers had made to hold in the water where they lived. The drop off was about five or six feet (1.5 to 1.82 meters) down or more, below that was water and on the other side of the narrow path was the water, it was almost level with the path we were walking along. The length of the path depended on how big the beaver dam was, usually about thirty to fifty feet (9.14 to 15.24 meters) across. You knew the water was deep and if a horse spooked or shied while on the path it would either fall down the steep bank or slip into the deep water. If that happened the horse would become tangled in all the branches under the water that held the dam together. Not a good outcome either way.

The most scary spot we encountered was when we had to cross the muskeg to get some stray cattle. Dad told me to go across first and to "give Volcano her head" (meaning not to guide her with the reins). He said that she would know where to step and not sink in the muskeg.

It was not uncommon for muskegs to be over 15 feet (4.57 meters) deep. We had heard that a large D-9 caterpillar tractor had sunk in a muskeg, never to be seen again.

I patted Volcano's neck and nudged her with my heels. She walked into the muskeg. Before we had ridden 10 feet (3.04 meters) we had sunk up to her shoulders. There was no way for us to turn around so I lifted my feet up and rested them on her back. Volcano pushed her way through the muskeg with the other horses following her path. Where we had to cross was probably 660 feet (301 meters) wide. I was never so glad to get to the other side and proud of my horse at the same time for showing up the other horses.

Everybody may laugh at her and say she is ugly, but she showed them all.
She showed them what she is made of.

I sat taller that day.

I kept Volcano for several years and we enjoyed many happy rides together.

The time that I spent on the backs of my horses, and the countless hours I sang "Amazing Grace" to God in the hopes that He would save me, and all of my secrets that I told them were the most memorable for me. All of these horses that were in my life helped me to keep my sanity. Without them, I am not sure how I would have survived the loneliness I felt. It did not matter if I was sitting on the ground in the middle of a field with them or riding in the lease all by myself. They were always there to protect me and to help me. I realized that God may not have been able to answer my prayers when I wanted to die but He did send me His horses. Thank God for His wisdom and guidance through the turmoil of my youth.

Horses will always be a part of my life. They are in my soul.

... the loners ...

I remember the year I was entering grade seven. It was daunting. I was now in junior high, but my grade was now located in the new high school. We were the little kids and it was always fun for the older students to pick on us. None of the older kids really bothered me, but the teachers sure did. I guess I was a bit too outspoken for them. I would tell them if they did something wrong or if they were picking on a certain student. This always landed me in trouble and at one time I was given the strap several times across my hands for being so outspoken against what I believed was abuse from the teacher toward a student in my class. The teacher had grabbed the kid by his ear and shook him because he was not listening to the instructions she was saying.

In my grade seven class there were two girls that did not have any friends. They were new to our school and I assumed that they had just moved to the area during the summer. None of the other students would talk to them, or even acknowledge that they existed. This behaviour from the other students towards those two girls, Mary and Carol, lasted through most of the school year. Mary eventually quit coming to school. As for Carol, her following year proved to be better because she found a friend.

Mary looked like she came from a poor family. She was a large girl about my height and wore a long skirt and button-down blouse. Her hair was long and stringy from not being washed regularly. I don't think that they had running water at her home.
Carol was the opposite in height, she was tall and gangly with short brown hair. She walked with her shoulders hunched because

of her height. She stood at least a foot taller than me. Her pants were always too short for her long legs and she wore sweaters all the time over top of a blouse.

During this time, I had taken to wearing my Dad's shirts to school with jeans and runners. Dad's shirt hung on me like a sack because I was only 14 years old and barely 90 lbs.

During every lunch break I would head to my favorite spot and sit by the hallway windows at the south entrance doors of our classroom wing. One day I noticed Mary slowly walking by with her head down. I called her name and she jerked her head and looked up at me with a startled look on her face. That startled look soon turned to fear. She was so used to people calling her names and picking on her, that she was not sure what to do when I said her real name.

She hesitated, and I waved her over, saying "It's okay, I just want to ask you something."

Mary replied, "What?"

I said, "For my class project for literature, I am writing a play about a stewardess on an airplane. Would you like to play a part in it?"

She looked rather shocked, swallowed and said: "Sure."

I needed one more actress for my play and a few moments later, Carol came walking from the other direction, and I called to her and asked the same question. She also said "Yes."

So for the next three weeks during lunch hour, the three of us wrote our screenplay for literature class. When it was due we acted out our parts in front of the whole class. I think it was a great project and we all had fun.

Throughout my junior and senior high school years I was always showing the kids that were less popular that someone cared that they existed. I wanted them to know that not all of the students were "clicky" or snobs. I was either giving someone my school lunch or hanging out with them for an afternoon. I always said "Hi" and acknowledged that they mattered, but I never became close friends with anyone. I did not want them to see me, I was afraid that they would know my secrets. I felt that if I let anyone close to me, they would see me for what had happened to me. Then they would also turn their backs on me, like I felt my family did.

I needed to keep the secrets under wraps and very, very guarded.

Some of the girls, during junior and senior high only wanted to be my friend so that they could get close to my one of my two brothers. These so called "friends of mine", would say that would like to spend the weekend at our farm riding the horses, but it did not take long for me to figure out that they wanted to come and see my brothers. That was how both of my brothers met their wives.

CHAPTER FOUR

... the memory...

I am not sure when the vision or image started to appear, I think it was when Nelson came back to visit. Every time I saw him, my body would tense up, my stomach would form knots in it, the hairs on my arms would stand on end, a shiver would run down my spine and a mini one or two second vision or image always flashed in my mind:

I am lying on my older brother's bed, my head is at the foot of the bed. My face is turned right; facing the closet.
My eyes are open but there is no life in them.
Nelson is on top of me, his pants are gone, and his penis is erect.
His arms are outstretched, he has one hand on each side of my head on the bed. There are cupboards above his head, the cupboards have curtains for doors. The closet has curtains for a door, the door frame to the room has curtains hanging for a door.
The house is quiet. I feel all alone.

By 1967, Dad had finished building Mom her dream house with four bedrooms, a big bathroom with a sink, tub and toilet in it, a big kitchen, with a separate living room and dining room area. Dad said that I could pick out my own bedroom first before any else, this I took to mean my brothers, because they were still going to be sharing a bedroom upstairs until Dad finished building Hank's bedroom in the basement. The new baby Mom was expecting would have the other bedroom that I did not choose for myself. I was so excited, no more sharing my room with Mom and Dad.

I have no memory of Nelson from the time I was five or six, until he brought home his girlfriend to meet my parents in 1968. I was outside with my brother Al playing on the lawn when Nelson and his girlfriend came outside. Nelson decided that he was going to horse around with us and he grabbed Al's arms and started to swing him around in a circle. Al's legs were off the ground. He looked like he was flying. When he was done spinning Al, then Nelson grabbed me by the wrists and spun me around. I'm not sure if I was enjoying myself.

I remember that I was facing the ground and it was spinning. Nelson was wearing black shiny shoes with brown pants. His girlfriend was clapping her hands together and laughing. My teeth were clenched tight and the skin on my wrists felt like it was being pulled off. I could not escape. That is the last time I remember seeing him, until his wedding day the following spring.

Over the years I knew things were not quite right about Nelson and how I felt about him. I felt that there was something wrong, but I had a hard time thinking what it could be. So over time I starting thinking that the "vision" I kept having had to be about Ted, and that I was doing what I called a "memory transfer" where I was putting Nelson in the image instead of Ted.

This was the only way that I could cope with the memory. But, I later found out that the mind will only let you do that for so long and then all hell breaks loose and you start to remember other things along with the memory to force you to accept the truth.

The next time I remember seeing Nelson, it was a warm spring day, and I was sitting in the pew of the small church, wearing a yellow dress with white lace over the top of it. The sleeves were see-through lace that came down to my elbows. I was wearing white gloves that ended at my wrists and wore pantyhose and black shiny shoes. My hair was curled in a bouffant hairdo with a yellow hairband in it. Mom and I were sitting in the fourth row of the church, and Dad stood at the back of the church.

The church seemed empty. Nelson and Marie were standing at the front of the church with the minister. I don't remember anybody else standing with them.

Sitting there watching Nelson and Marie get married I had the vision, the memory again:

*I am lying on my older brother's bed, my head is at the foot of the
bed. My face is turned right; facing the closet.
My eyes are open but there is no life in them.
Nelson is on top of me, his pants are gone, and his penis is erect.
His arms are outstretched, he has one hand on each side of my
head on the bed. There are cupboards above his head, the
cupboards have curtains for doors. The closet has curtains for a
door, the door frame to the room has curtains hanging for a door.
The house is quiet. I feel all alone.*

I did not understand why I was seeing that image.

... loneliness ...

In the fall of 1967 my two brothers and I had joined the 4-H beef club. 4-H was an organization where you took a calf that had been born that spring, fed it all winter, groomed it, and taught it to lead. In June, the following spring, you had an Achievement Day. All of the 4-H Beef clubs from all of the nearby surrounding communities would arrive at the local Auction Market to compete in classes from grooming to showmanship. After everyone had competed with their steers and the public speaking and judging classes were finished, then you sold your steer through an auction sale.

After we sold our steers we would then deposit the profits from the sale into the bank. We could use the money on whatever we wanted: I used mine to try and save my sanity. I was in 4-H for five years.

It was after the first year that I had been in 4-H, when I started to walk downtown every day during the school lunch hour and take one dollar out of my savings account. With that one dollar I would go to the Tomboy Store and buy a box of Old Dutch potato chips. In each box you got three bags of chips.

Mom packed us school lunches every day. Most days it was bologna or Spam (processed meat in a can with jelled fat stuck to it) sandwiches, two jumbo raisin cookies and an apple or orange. I rarely ate my lunches. I hated Spam and bologna and jumbo cookies, and I rarely ate fruit, as I didn't like the taste. I would give my lunches to some kid that did not have a lunch to eat. I never threw it away. Instead, for my lunch I would eat a bag of potato chips that I had bought. Then when I got home, instead of eating supper with the rest of the family, I would stay in my room and eat another bag of chips for my supper. I lived on Old Dutch potato chips for about four straight years.

The reason that I stared eating the potato chips for supper was so that I would not have to do the dishes. I thought that if I did not eat at home then I would not have to do the dishes; I would not have to stand at the counter; I would not be vulnerable again. But it didn't work that way. Mom told me that even if I did not eat supper I still had to do the dishes. So nearly every night when everyone sat down at supper, I would stay in my room and eat a bag of chips. When supper was finished, Mom would yell for me to clear the table and to dry the dishes. I would come out of my room only then and when I was finished with the dishes, I would go back into my room until the next morning when I had to go to school.

Years later, when I finally started to eat supper again with the rest of the family on a regular basis, right after finishing supper I would get severe cramps, feel clammy and sweaty and I would have to go to the washroom. Dad would yell at me to get out of the bathroom and to help with the dishes. When I came out of the bathroom I was still shaking and having a hard time breathing.

I am not sure why he cared, I always had to do them anyhow, sooner or later. I am sure that because Mom and I fought about the dishes all the time Dad thought that it was just another attempt of mine to get out of them, after all I was lazy (or so they said).

I know now that the stomach cramps were a product of a psychological effect from the trauma I had suffered as a child. I know now that it had all started because I was left in the house to dry the dishes and Ted attacked me. I had at a very early age associated dishes with Ted.

After I was out living on my own, I never had a problem doing my own dishes. In fact I hate dirty dishes. I would rather wash them by hand than use a dishwasher. That doesn't sound like someone who hates dishes and is lazy.

As a child, I was terrified to stand at the counter and do the dishes. I always felt vulnerable. I would get goose bumps all over my body and feel uncomfortable. How could I ever tell them that? What would they have said? I think that they would have said that I was making it up so that I could get out of chores.

... 1970, the end of the baby ...

For years, I used to wonder how I was going tell Mom and Dad that I was going to have a baby. I knew that when bulls bred a cow she had a calf later. I had seen all the other animals breed and later have babies, so I figured that I was going to have a baby too sometime. But when?

It haunted me every day. I was so confused about everything regarding how a girl should feel or act. Finally it happened: I woke up in the middle of the night in absolute agony. I thought for sure that I was finally having the baby. I was scared and in a lot of pain. My mind was racing again.

How am I going to tell everyone, who's going to believe me? Oh God, they will hate me more. Finally Mom will be able to send me away.

I managed to get out of bed and make it to the bathroom. I closed the door and went to sit on the toilet. Then I saw the blood. I doubled over again from the cramping. My back felt like someone was trying to break it in half. I sat there on the toilet rocking back and forth and moaning in pain, doubled over with my hands pushing hard against my stomach, resting my forehead on my knees. The sweat was dripping off my forehead, and my body felt clammy and cold.

Is this what it feels like to die?

Flashback to 1968, when I was eleven:

Mom is standing in the living room ironing clothes.
I had finally gotten the courage up to tell her what had happened
to me, to tell her about Ted.
I swallowed hard and walked over to her. Her back was to me. I
was nervous and scared. I did not know what she would do. I
hoped that she would turn around and hug me and tell me that
everything was okay. That she would say that she cared about me,
that she really did love me.
I knew I could not say Ted's name out loud, I knew I was still
afraid that he would kill my family,
so I said "Mom, the boy fucked me."
I thought if I had not said his name out loud then he could not
blame me when they found out what he did to me.

Mom didn't even look up from the clothes she was ironing. She
simply said, "That is what you get when you play with boys."
I don't think she really understood what I had said.

I stand there for a minute staring at my feet thinking "It's all my
fault. I caused this to happen."
I turned around and walked out of the house. I am in a daze. I feel
so totally alone and lost.
My shoulders feel so heavy. My heart feels heavy. It is so hard to
breath.

As I was sitting there in the bathroom, I heard the door open. I
looked over to see Mom standing there in her pink housecoat. She
walked over to the bottom cupboard and pulled out a sanitary pad
and belt and handed it to me without a word, then left.

At that moment I realized that I was not having a baby then. But
when?

I entered grade eight a few months later, the terrible cramping had
only happened that one night. It was in my first health class that
the penny finally dropped. I learned the difference between boys
and girls, and that it took only nine months to grow a baby. I also

finally figured out what the cramping was all about and the pad with the belt mom had handed me.

I felt so stupid for thinking that I was having a baby, but I also felt a huge weight lifted off my shoulders at the same time.

That was a great day! I was giddy and happy. I had lots of fun that day. I walked a little lighter. I laughed a little louder. I felt like shouting to the world: "I AM NOT GOING TO HAVE A BABY!" One more demon was laid to rest that day.

... never again ...

Three months had passed by, Mom and Dad were having a Christmas Party or New Year's Eve party for a bunch of friends. The rule was: adults upstairs, kids under 18 downstairs.

During the party, I decided that I was going to be the bartender for the adults. *Every bartender should take pride in their work*, I thought. So I sampled every drink I poured from Baby Duck to Lonesome Charlie wine to hard liquor drinks like rye and coke, vodka and orange juice, etc.

Soon a sip here and a sip there left me in a very happy staggering mood. It didn't dawn on me that I could get drunk from taking those little sips. As the night progressed, one could say so did I. Soon the alcohol had taken over my brain. I can't say that I was a terrible drunk, but I sure was a frustrated one. It did not take long for the problems that I was recently having with Mom to come tumbling to the surface. All night I kept mumbling to the other kids there: "I didn't break the chandelier."

Around the previous July, I was looking after Dottie and she was playing on the living room with her hula hoop, swinging it around. I told her to quit swinging it in the air because she was going to hit the new chandelier that Grandma had given Mom and Dad for the new house. But Dottie would not listen to me, and the hula hoop hit the bottom of the chandelier, breaking the crystal ball hanging down. When Mom came home and found the chandelier busted, she asked me "What on earth happened?" I replied to her, "Dottie broke it"

"Liar!" Mom said "Don't you try to blame your sister!"

Mom made sure that she told anyone that came over to the house for a visit what had happened to the chandelier. She would say to them, "Grandma had sent us this beautiful chandelier for our living room as a house warming gift and within days of putting it up, Brenda broke it and then she tried to blame her little sister."

I think she had this rehearsed, for she said the same thing every time. The company's response was also always the same.

The neighbours said, "Oh no, how terrible, what are you going to do with her?"

Mom always said in reply, "I don't know what I will do with her, she is so hard to control. I don't know what I ever did to deserve a child like her."

At any rate, I was getting pretty drunk at the party, so my brother, Al, his girlfriend and his best friend decided that they needed to get me outside and take me for a walk down the road to try and sober me up. I was not very cooperative with this plan. I kept tripping and falling down. I guess they then decided that maybe plunking me onto a haystack in the backyard would be a better idea.

Finally I decided that I was cold and I staggered back to the house where it was warm. I managed to get into the house and stumbled back down the basement stairs where I landed on Nelson's velvet couch and threw up.

Newlyweds, Nelson and Marie had stored the couch in my parents' basement as they had no room at their house for it at the time. For some reason, it felt really good to puke on Nelson's precious couch. Besides, it made my stomach feel slightly better too.

Later Nelson came downstairs to see what we were up to. He noticed the puke on his couch. Boy, was he mad! He turned to look at all of us and screeched, "Who puked on my antique couch?" Everyone pointed at me and said that I was drunk. Nelson stomped over to me and grabbed me by the arm and dragged me back to the couch. He glared at me and through clenched teeth snarled, "You had better clean up this mess you little bitch! Wait until I tell your Mom that you are drunk."

I looked up at him. The room was spinning, and it was hard to focus on him. I said, "I don't give a damn!"

Nelson dropped my arm and stomped back up the stairs.

Suddenly I panicked my mind started to race, *No wait, I can't be drunk, I must get my body to work, I must get my brain to work, I must save myself.*
Oh who cares, nobody cares about me, what difference does it make? Nobody cares that I'm drunk, they won't even notice.
NO, stop it, must save myself, must think clearly, have to hide. Can't think.

All that night as I kept drinking, I continued to mumble about not breaking the chandelier. I sounded like a broken record. I needed someone to believe me, anyone.

The following morning Mom opened my bedroom door. I was lying on the bed with my head slightly over the edge of the bed facing the door. Mom stood there and said "Serves you right for being drunk! If you puke in your room and on your bed you WILL clean it up yourself."

I looked at her with as much malice as I could muster at that moment and slurred, "I did not break the chandelier." Mom just looked at me in disgust and shut the door. I could hear mumbling coming from the kitchen, then the voices rose a bit and I heard my name. Dad had heard that I kept saying that I didn't break the chandelier. He also had heard that Dottie had broken it from the neighbor kids (who had been there at the time, but were too afraid to tell Mom the truth). He realized that Mom had blamed me unjustly. Mom never did apologize to me, but I didn't hear about the chandelier again or hear the story told.

I was violently ill for four days. My head was pounding so hard that I thought it was going to break, my mouth was dry and it felt like my tongue was swollen. I could not get my eyes to focus on anything in my room. They hurt from the light, it appeared that they had their own will and would roll into the back of my head, into the darkness there. I could barely move my body and getting out of bed was nearly impossible. Nothing in my body wanted to work no matter how hard I tried to will it to work. My legs were so weak and shaky they would not hold me up and I had to crawl to the bathroom next door to my room. Doing that would cause my body to start shaking and break out in a cold sweat. Once in the bathroom I would just lay there on the floor for a while waiting for the room to quit moving, then I would lift myself up high enough to throw up in the toilet. Eventually I would make it back to my room and collapse on the bed. I thought that I was dying a very slow and painful death.

Mom never came in to see me during those four days. She left me alone. Maybe she was hoping that I would just die and be done with it. Then she would not have to be bothered with me anymore.

About a week later I cleaned off the "antique" couch.

For the next five years my body could no longer fight the stress it was under. My immune system was not working very well and I contracted every flu that came around, I had the measles, chest and head colds, and cold sores in abundance. When I had the various flus I would be down and out from four to seven days unable to eat anything and barely could drink water. I could not keep on any weight, not that I was heavy, but my backbone stuck out of my back about half an inch. I was a walking skeleton.

I am not sure how I feel when I re-live that night and its aftermath. I know that I can feel that heavy feeling in my chest, the utter loneliness. Thank goodness I don't feel the stomach sickness also. When I think about it now, I am amazed that I did not die from alcohol poisoning.

To this day, I do not really drink. I learned my lesson: alcohol does not make anything go away, no matter how much you drink. I also learned that I needed to be in control of my senses at all times. I needed to be able to count on my body to escape and I needed my mind to be able to think fast. I had to stay on guard for Ted, for anything, for anyone that might hurt me. My survival depended on it.

... am i finally saved?...

I was sixteen and had just gotten my driver's license.

For the past week the "Crusade for Christ" had been in town.
Several of my school acquaintances were involved in the program
and said that it was fun. It was the last day of the Crusade for
Christ, so I decided to go and see what it was all about. I asked
Dad if I could borrow the car to go to the Crusade, then I phoned
the neighbour girls, Anna and Leigh and asked if they wanted to go
with me.

As I mentioned previously, Anna and Leigh were four and six
years younger than me. I was their babysitter, and wild older
friend.

Although Anna and Leigh attended the Catholic church almost
every Sunday, they never ever tried to save me as their church
project. I had always been the Baptist neighbours' church project.
It was their intention to try to save the heathen child. I had heard
that phrase, "heathen child`` many times over the years and was
sick of it. Anyways, I was not going to let them use me as a project
any more. Throughout my youth, I had been invited by the local
neighbor kids to almost every church in town, this usually
happened when they had a drive on to find new members or as a
Sunday school project where they received points by bringing in
new people to save. I knew that these people were never concerned
about me, they were only interested in getting the most points and
winning their contests. But I didn't mind most of the time, it got
me out of the house.

When Anna, Leigh and I arrived at the Catholic school where the Crusade was being held, I parked the car and we went in. I decided that we would sit in the first three seats of the third row. As the choir was getting ready to sing, I noticed that a few of my school acquaintances were in the choir, along with a male and a female bus driver, who had each caused problems for me over the years.

The two bus drivers took turns operating the school bus. I had the most trouble with him. According to him, I was a heathen and should be punished because I would not bow down to his abuse and small-mindedness.

I made me sick to look at those two people standing there, all smug and righteous, acting better than me. I could not help but think what hypocrites they were. I knew that they were not good Christians. I knew that they were hypocrites and not at all what good Christians are supposed to be like. I knew that you should treat others the way you wanted to be treated and that you should never make assumptions about others.

In all those years of Sunday school and various churches I learned: "You should not condemn thy neighbour until you have walked a mile in their shoes." They had definitely not walked in my shoes.

To me, Christianity was in your heart, and you lived it every day. I felt that I did not need to go to church like they did to be a good Christian. Hanging on our kitchen wall beside the door was a plaque of the Ten Commandments. Every day I read it and tried to live my life that way. Not every day was a perfect day, but I still tried. Besides, look what going to church did to them, they thought that they were better than everyone else. They acted like they were God, passing judgement on people that they did not really know.

When the show was nearly over, the preacher asked if anyone in the audience would like to be saved and to join the world of Christians. I thought to myself that maybe this was my chance to be saved. I told Anna and Leigh that I was going to see what all the fuss was about, and they decided to join me.

I never told them that I truly wanted to be saved and hopefully, by some miracle, to have Ted put behind me. I could not tell them that, for I had never told a soul. Only God knew why I wanted to be saved, and tonight could be the night that it was finally over.

I hoped that since one of the girls in the choir had been saved, why not me? She was a very sexually promiscuous young lady and had been seeing boys in the basement under the school gymnasium.

After we had all walked out of the gym to be saved, we were split up. A lady came and sat with me and started to read scriptures from the Bible. She didn't ask why I thought I should be saved; she was too wrapped up in reading her script that was provided for her. She never talked to me, she just rambled on. She never looked at me, never saw who was sitting in front of her. I was just another person to add to the list of Christians, another quota that was being filled.

When the "saving session" was over, everyone was sent back into the gym where this time we were welcomed back as Christians. The two bus drivers came over to me and said that they were sorry for all the years that they had given me problems on the school bus.

They looked at me and said "You are a Christian now," and "You have been saved and are now in the family of the Lord."

I looked at the both of them and replied "I am still the same person that I was when I walked in here two hours ago. I have not changed."

I stood there looking at these hypocrites. They did not care about me. They did not care about why I thought I needed to be saved. They did not care to know, they only thought that I was a heathen.

I knew that I had not been saved, and I turned from them and walked away. We left the school and drove home. During the drive I asked the two girls if they had been saved. They said that the people that they were sitting with had only read a few scriptures from the Bible and then told them that they were saved. The person that read to me had not told me that I was saved. Why? That familiar feeling of isolation and loneliness was coming home to rest once again. How was I ever going to be able to put Ted behind me? Why couldn't I find a way to do that? What was wrong?

After dropping off the girls at their place, I slowly drove back home. I knew that I had not been saved and I kept thinking over and over: *Why? Why was everyone else able to be saved and not me? Why couldn't the nice neighbour lady from years ago save me, and why couldn't the Crusade for Christ save me?*

I was probably around 12 when I started visiting the neighbor lady up the road about a one and half miles from us. I called her Mrs. G. She was about fifty or sixty, and she had three children that rode on the same school bus as me. I remember her daughter was quite a bit older than me, and beautiful. She had long black wavy hair, large eyes, and smooth skin. She was very quiet. During the year that she rode the bus I would sit in my seat just behind her on the opposite side and just stare at her. I was mesmerized by what she looked like and how she carried herself: so elegant; so pure.

One afternoon Mrs. G had just gotten back from church and was telling me about a revival that she had gone to. She said the minister was walking around and healing and saving people by just touching them. She told me that it was amazing how people were being saved from their illnesses and sins. I was intrigued and asked her if she could save me.

So the next day, I jumped on my bike and headed to Mrs. G's house to be saved. I was excited and could not pedal my bike fast enough to get there. When I arrived, Mrs. G took me into her dining room and asked me to sit down on her wooden kitchen chair. She then stood behind me and asked me to relax and close my eyes. I promptly closed my eyes, but the relaxing part was a bit harder as I did not know how to relax. I could feel the sun warming my face as it shone through her dining room windows, and eventually my mind drifted away and soon my shoulders slumped.

Mrs. G put her hands on the top of my hand and started to chant, then she chanted louder and louder. Pretty soon she started to move my head sideways, like she was trying to shake the devil out as she chanted. As my head was being frantically jerked all over she said, "Do you feel it, do you feel it coming?"

I was not sure what I was supposed to feel so I said, "No."

She then asked, "Do you feel it in your arm? I feel it coming through your arm. Do you feel it now?"

Not sure what to say and thinking that my arm was starting to hurt I said, "Yes, I can feel it in my arm." She chanted louder and suddenly let my head go with such force that I almost hit it on the table.

When I recovered and sat back up straight, Mrs. G was sitting next to me on a wooden chair. She turned to me, took my hands in hers and said, "My child you are healed."

I rode home on my bike, knowing that I had not been saved, that my arm was only hurting because it was banging on the table while she was jerking my head all over the place. I did not want to disappoint Mrs. G. and tell her that I was not saved.

Was it because I was not worth saving?

I talked to God all the time, I even sang his hymn, "Amazing Grace" when I was out on my horse. I would sing at the top of my lungs:

> Amazing Grace, how sweet the sound,
> That saved a wretch like me.
> I once was lost, but now I am found,
> Was blind but now I see.
> Amazing Grace, how sweet the sound,
> That saved a wretch like me.
> I once was lost, but now I am found,
> Was blind but now I see.
> Amazing Grace, how sweet the sound,

That saved a wretch like me.
I once was lost, but now I am found,
Was blind but now I see.
Amazing Grace, how sweet the sound,
That saved a wretch like me.
I once was lost, but now I am found,
Was blind but now I see.

I especially liked the part in the song about "saving a wretch like me," so I sang this part a bit louder than the rest. I wanted to make sure that God heard what I was saying, and what I was asking him, and praying that he would do it.

Why was I not worth saving? Was I that bad? Why? Oh God! Why?

CHAPTER FIVE

... has God finally sent me my relief? ...

It was a fall night, the moon was full and the skies were clear. It was in the wee hours of the morning and everyone in the house was asleep. I was sleeping in my room beside the bathroom. I am not sure what made me wake up, but when I did, I was lying on my right side facing the window. I opened my eyes and saw the shadow of a man standing over me with a knife in his hand. All I could see was the reflection of the blade gleaming in the moonlight. The man was holding the knife over his head. I watched the reflection of the blade as he moved it from side to side. I lay there not moving, my heart pounding in my chest, slowly breathing watching the motion of the knife with my eyes. I couldn't see his face, only the blade of the knife.

I thought: *Should I scream or something? But if I scream he might kill everyone else in the house while they're sleeping. If he's in my room, he's here for a reason. Maybe he's going to stab me with the knife. Thank God someone is going to end my pitiful existence!"*

So I closed my eyes and breathed a sigh of relief knowing that my escape was finally here. The only thoughts that ran through my head as I waited for the end to come were:

No more Ted.
No more feeling empty.
No more being alone.
No more being different.
No more running and hiding.
No more being terrified.
No more feeling that there's something else that I just can't remember.

No more being afraid of what I can't remember.
My family will be better off without me.
How can they like me if I don't like myself?
My God, how could they love me?
How could anyone love me?
It'll be better this way.
They'll all be much better off.
I'm too much trouble.
No more Ted,
Thank God, no more Ted.

As you can guess the man did not stab me to death that night. It was probably a dream or an illusion. I am not sure if I felt relieved or sad about that.

… was it a coincidence or a premonition? …

Several days later, everyone was sitting at the breakfast table. There was a news bulletin announced over the radio that two convicts had escaped from the nearby Correctional Institution. They were still at large. Police were warning everyone to be on the lookout and to lock their doors at night.

We never locked our door. Nobody was ever around at night. We knew all of our neighbours and we lived too far out of town for anyone to bother us. My parents said that there were several farms closer to town, and that those people would be hit first. Nobody was worried.

The next day a friend of mine named Ursula was over. She was spending the weekend with me, well actually she had a crush on my brother and that is really who she was there to see.

Again it was in the middle of the night and everyone was sleeping. A rustling noise coming from the porch woke me up. I turned over to see if Ursula had woken up from the noise, but she was still sound asleep.
I woke her up and whispered to her, "Did you hear anything?"

She said "No."

We lay there listening, but she said that she couldn't hear anything and rolled over and went back to sleep.

I lay there for a minute wondering if I was hearing things. I wondered if the man had come back to finally finish the job from the night before. I looked at Ursula sleeping there and I realized, *He can't stab me tonight. If he comes back into my room then he will have to kill her too.* I started to feel panic slowly flooding my body again and settling in my chest. Once again my mind was racing at full speed:

I have to protect her; I have to protect my family.
He will stab everyone, there will be blood everywhere, and they will all suffer because of me.
Dottie is too little to die, she has not even begun her life; it wouldn't be fair to her. Hank should live too.
Al and Ursula would not have a happy life because of me. Dad and Mom work hard to feed us and give us a home; they don't deserve to die, especially because of me. I am such a disappointment to them both. God I wish Mom would love me like she loves everyone else!
They will all die and it will be my fault. Everyone will blame me; everyone will know how terrible I am. It is not their fault that Ted wouldn't leave me alone, it was my fault. Mom said so. I remember when I tried to tell her what had happened and she said that it was my fault.
I can't let them all die because of me, I have to protect them.

I slowly slid out of bed and crept down the hall. I kept my back against the wall, and peeked around the edge of the fridge into the porch. At the bottom of the steps leading into the porch, two men were standing there whispering to themselves. They didn't seem to know that I was there. I slowly backed away from the fridge and crept back down the hall to Mom's and Dad's bedroom.

I gently shook Dad to wake him up and whispered that there were two men standing in the porch. He quickly got out of bed, pulled on his pants and headed down the hallway to the kitchen and turned on the light. He confronted the men and asked them what they were doing in our house. I stayed standing at the edge of the fridge watching the two men and Dad. Mom went to wake up Hank and Al. The two men told Dad that they needed a lift to town because their car had broken down and they had walked to the nearest farm. Dad told them to wait in the porch, while he got ready to drive them into town. I still stayed by the fridge, watching them. When Hank came into the kitchen he took the two men outside and waited for Dad to come. Before leaving, Dad grabbed his revolver and stuffed it in his shirt, then he headed down the steps and out the door. Everyone waited until Dad and Hank got back.

When they finally got back home, Dad told Mom that there was no car broken down on the road where the men said it was.

I thought to myself: *Everyone is safe again, I protected them from the men.*

I do not know if these men were the escaped convicts or not, but after that night the outside door was always locked at night.

I guessed that my time was not up yet. I didn't know if I should be happy or sad. I guessed that I was happy because I was alive, but sad because Ted was still there with me in my thoughts. I could still feel the heaviness in my shoulders and chest, and sometimes if felt so hard to breathe. I was still dirty, still ugly, and still all by myself. Maybe this was how I was supposed to feel?

... don't trust them ...

When I first started to consider going out on dates, I would make sure that I always had a friend with me. I was never alone with the guy in the beginning until I knew for sure that it was safe.

To me, young men were only interested in one thing: having sex, and having it with as many girls as possible.

I already had my fill of being used as a little child, and so I would watch out for the guys who did not care about girls and only wanted sex from them. I was not lining up for that "smuck truck." Unfortunately, having only experience with abusive behaviour to draw from and a family that never spoke the "S" word in the house, my judgements about what the guys I did date wanted was a bit distorted, to say the least.

I joined the dating game in the spring of grade 10, after I had returned home from a school trip to England.

It seems like I never had a problem attracting guys. There was this one particular grade 12 guy that had a definite crush on me. Will would leave notes on my locker telling me how much he liked me. He waited for me at my locker between classes. Many times I was late for class because Will was standing there waiting for me. I would wait until he finally left for his class before going to my locker. Finally I got wise and started to carry most of my books for my morning classes or afternoon classes with me.

Whenever Will managed to track me down, he would suggest that we should go out on a date. I never did date him, nor did I give him any indication that I was interested. To me, he only wanted one thing, and he was not going to get it from me.

I had joined the high school travel club that year and for Easter break we were heading to England and some students were also travelling to Paris. Will was also going to England with the group of students from grade twelve. Funny, it was easier to keep a distance from him in England then it was at home. I'm pretty sure that he had plans for us to get together while in Europe, but I stopped that pretty quickly. I thanked him for asking me out but emphasized that I was not interested in dating anyone. Will got the hint and never bothered me again.

I suppose if I had just told him to bugger off in the beginning, he would have left, but I could not hurt his feelings. After all, I knew what that felt like and did not want to deliberately do that to anyone. I felt that if I had liked someone enough to put my feelings on the line, I would not like to have someone step on them. I was so afraid of hurting other peoples' feelings that I never thought much about my own. That is not to say I was a door mat, I definitely knew how to verbally scrap if I was forced to. But on the whole, I tried to avoid conflict.

It was the summer holidays and this particular day was a scorcher. I had just come out of the house when a blue truck pulled into our yard and parked in front of the house. Paul had stopped in to see me "out of the blue" so to speak.

Paul was a very good looking guy with black curly hair and deep brown eyes. He had just graduated from grade 12. I guess you could say that he had been flirting with me between classes during the last trimester of school.

Paul wanted me to go with him and his friend Dave to the lake. He told me several times that he thought I was really cute and would like to get to know me better. I was not worried about Dave, he had a girlfriend already, but I did not really know Paul, so I told him that I could not go. Paul said, "That's too bad, it could have been fun." He never asked me again to go out on a date.

I always wondered what it would have been like to go with Paul. Would I have had a nice time? Fear would not let me go out with anyone. I was terrified to go with them by myself. I figured that if I was alone with them then something would happen to me, but if I had a friend with me then I would be safe.

I felt so totally useless. I couldn't even go out on a date. What was wrong with me? I hated myself for being so scared.

I finally did start to date a young man named Jim when I was 17 years old. He was young, tall, blonde and very sure of himself. I felt that he was not dating me just to try to get into my pants. I thought, *finally someone who wants me for me, not like the boys in our school who are on a mission to score*. I felt safe dating someone who did not go to school anymore, someone with a steady job, someone responsible. Someone who wasn't only interested in sex but wanted a more meaningful relationship.

Over the years, I have slowly come to realize that a lot of good young men wanted to date me, and yes, more than likely to try to develop a relationship which did include being intimate. I was terrified of these young men, but they were not axe murderers and social deviants. They were mostly young men looking to experience the dating game, and hopefully to find that special someone to share their life with.

My childhood had been robbed from me and now my teenage years were drastically altered because of my abusers.

... he seems different ...

When I first saw Jim, he was at the local movie theater with his pregnant girlfriend. I was around 14 years old at the time, and for some reason I could not take my eyes off of him. He seemed so caring with her. He got her popcorn and pop and sat with his arm around her during the show.

I thought to myself as I stared at him: *WOW, this man loves this woman. Someday I am going to find that special person too. But how? I am scared and ugly. Who on God's green earth would want me? He would see into my soul and know that he was not the first person I've been with sexually. I am damaged goods.*

Three years later when I was 17, Jim and I started dating. At first, whenever we had a date, I would drag my two neighbors Anna and Leigh with me. Jim must have thought that I was crazy to bring along my neighbors, but I always told him that I was babysitting. The two girls would sit in the backseat of his car while I sat in the front with him and away we would go.
In the beginning, our dates would consist of going to the Pacific 66 truck stop in town for a coke, or sometimes we would go to the lake for the afternoon.

Anna and Leigh loved his speed boat and loved riding in it! Jim seemed to enjoy showing off his boat to everyone.

I am really not sure why Jim was interested in me. After all, I had to have other people with me on our dates. At the beginning of our dating, Jim and I were never alone together.

Finally school started back in September, and Anna and Leigh could no longer be my excuse for not being alone with him. Every lunch hour he would drive by the school and pick me up. Sometimes Ursula came along, but that was mostly so that Jim could drive her out to the farm to drop her off to see my brother Al. If Jim was not working, he would pick me up after school and drive me home.

In the two and a half years that we dated, I never really went out to parties with him. Nearly all of our dates were spent alone together, either going to a show or driving to Grande Prairie. Jim's job required him to work on 8 hour shifts in a gas/sulfur plant that was about 15 miles out of town, so we did not see each other all of the time. Usually we dated once a week when he was working nights and several times a week if he was on days.

Jim never drank when I was with him and we never saw any of his other friends. This arrangement suited me fine. I was not comfortable around people that I did not know. One of his old girlfriends did not like him dating me, and would always tell me what I was doing wrong and that she knew him better than anyone. I thought, *if that's true, then why is he dating me and not her?*

Our relationship was a bit stormy at times. It seemed that we broke up more times than we were together. Whenever I met someone else during one of our breakups, Jim would make sure that he was back in the picture. He would phone all the time, and stop by the house unannounced. Jim was always trying to break up the new relationship. He succeeded each time.

... he seems nice and safe ...

In between one of Jim's and my many break ups, Alfred entered the picture. I was walking to Jim's house from the High School to pick up a pair of shoes that I had left there. Alfred stopped and offered to give me a ride.

I had first met Alfred a few years earlier when he would come down to the farm to do weight lifting in our basement with Hank and few other friends.

Alfred and Jim had gone to school together and there was apparently no love lost between the two. Jim always had girlfriends, a nice car, and money. Alfred, on the other hand, was everybody's big brother, and had an old beat up car and very little money. Alfred spent most of his money on booze. He loved to party every weekend and get drunk. It appeared that Alfred did not have many dates. All of the girls thought of him as a brother and not a serious prospect to date.

Alfred and I were an unlikely couple. I was not a drinker and would never ride with someone who had been drinking if I could help it. It was not uncommon for me on a date to have one drink and sip at it all night long by adding pop or ice to it.

In the beginning Alfred would ask me to go out with him only when he knew that I had to babysit Dottie. I guess he was always afraid that I would reject him, and this gave him an excuse for being turned down.

I always had a difficult time babysitting Dottie at night, because I was always afraid to be in the house alone. I would hear every crack and groan the house would make and would sit terrified with fear that someone was in the basement. Man, if I could have, I would have left the house and hid outside, but I could not leave Dottie alone in the house nor could I take her outside in the middle of the night.

One day Alfred has asked if I would go to the dance with him the following Saturday night. I did not have any plans nor was I watching Dottie. So I told him "Yes." Saturday night came and I was sitting at the kitchen table all dressed up waiting. I was watching the traffic go by on the road, waiting to see if one of the cars turned on their signal light to indicate they were coming to our house. Alfred was late, so when he finally phoned, I asked him where he was. He said that he had just picked up his date and asked me to tell Hank that he would meet him at the dance. I told him that he was an asshole and hung up the phone. I stayed home that night, stewing, thinking that I should not be surprised, after all who would want to date me? A few days later, he told me that his date had ditched him at the dance and went home with another guy. I told him that he deserved it for asking me to the dance then not showing up.

When Alfred and I finally did start dating, I made it very clear to him that I was not going to be having sex with him at all. I was not going to be a notch on his belt. I wanted him to like me for my mind and not my body.

Hank was furious when he found out that Alfred was going to be dating his sister. He called me a slut and a whore and said that I should leave his best friend alone. I guess Hank did not want to lose his drinking buddy. Unfortunately they did not remain very close after that. Alfred apparently wanted to date me more than he wanted to go out to parties and get drunk. Because I refused to ride with him when he had been drinking, he made the attempt to not drink much when I was with him. When he drank too much or it looked like it was going to be getting out of control I would have him take me home. If he was going to kill himself as a drunk driver, I was not going to be in the car with him. After dropping me off, Alfred would head back to the party and get drunk.

Alfred was very possessive and hated it if another guy talked to me or even looked at me. It did not matter if it was an old school friend, or not. If the person talking happened to be a male, Alfred was angry. He would stay mad at me for hours and sometimes days. I had to make sure that no one talked to me or came near me when Alfred was around. I did not want him to be angry.

It was the beginning of summer, and Alfred and I had been dating for 6 months. I was getting ready to leave for summer school in Edmonton. I wanted to finish high school sooner than later so that I could move out of my parents' house and leave town. I had also had enough of Alfred and told him that his possessive behaviour was driving me crazy and that I did not want to date him anymore. I told him that he was too possessive and controlling and that I needed some space from him. He did not take the news well. I was glad that I was leaving home for most of the summer. Over two hundred miles and over a four hour drive was as far away as I could get.

I was running away and hiding, a definite pattern that had followed me through my childhood and now it was following me through my teenage years.

I did not want to have to face Alfred every day, I knew that I was not strong enough to fight him, my family and my friends, all of whom were definitely pissed at me for breaking up with him. They all told me that I was a bitch for hurting his feelings. I guess I was stupid to think that my feelings should count.

... trying to escape ...

Going to summer school would take me away to Edmonton for six weeks during the summer holidays, away from the farm and away from Alfred. It would also allow me to finish grade 12 in five months instead of ten. I would be able to move out of the house. I would be free, I thought, no more running, no more hiding, no more escaping.

Ursula had also decided to go to summer school, so we were going to stay with her sister and friend at their apartment. The apartment had only two bedrooms, so I was to sleep on the couch. Kay and Gail had two male friends, Pete and Edward, who always came over, visiting with them. They soon became friends with us too, since we saw them nearly every night.

We had been in the city for several weeks, going to school Monday to Friday and then catching the Greyhound bus back home every Friday night. We spent the weekends at the farm, then headed back to the city Sunday night. One night Edward asked if I would like to go to the "Klondike Days" exhibition on the weekend with him. I thought that it would be okay. After all, I had seen him every night visiting Gail and Kay for the past several weeks. He seemed like a nice guy and I did not think that the ladies would have bad friends. So I stayed in Edmonton that weekend.

When Ursula had arrived home late Friday night for the weekend, she told my Mom that I was going out on a date instead of coming home. Mom was furious! On the Saturday morning, she phoned me and told me that I should have come home, and that if I got into trouble then I deserved it.

Ursula had Al to go home for. I did not have anyone to go home to. If anyone cared that I did not come home, it was only because they had no one else to do the housework. It certainly was not because they missed me, nobody ever missed me.

Late Saturday afternoon Edward and Pete arrived at the apartment to pick me up to go to Klondike Days. I had no idea that Edward did not own a vehicle and that Pete was dropping us off at the grounds. Edward and I spent some time going on the rides (which did not sit with me too well) and then he went to play some of the games where you could win a stuffed animal. He told me that he wanted to win a stuffed teddy bear for his ex-girlfriend. When he told me that, I told him that he could take me back to the apartment. I said that he should go see his ex-girlfriend if he missed her that much.

I thought, *What a crappy date!*

I was thinking that once I got back to the apartment I was going to relax and watch some TV, then go to bed. I had some studying that I had to do and this was going to be a good weekend by myself. Call me naïve, but I did not even have Kay's address and trusted that Edward knew it. He did know it, but didn't have any intentions of telling me. Instead he took me back to his house. To this day I have no idea where it was.

At his house we started talking about my ex-boyfriend Jim. He asked me if I had a child with him. I told him he was crazy, why would I do that? The next thing I knew Edward was all over me. I told him that he could take me back to the apartment, he told me that he might take me later if I was really good.

I had nowhere to go, it was dark outside and I had no clue where I was. There was no one I could call to help me. Kay and Gail had also gone away for the weekend. I could not call the police to come and help me, I did not even know the address where I was or of the apartment I was staying at. I was all alone.

Edward became very forceful in what he wanted. I told him that I had my period. I figured that he would not try anything with me then. Boy, was I wrong!

He raped me four times that night. I was afraid that the tampon I was wearing would get pushed up inside me and I would not be able to get it out. He did not care that I had my period, he did not care that I tried to struggle free and screamed "No!" He did not care about me, he only wanted to use me. Finally in the morning he called a cab, gave the driver the address and sent me back to the apartment. I never saw him again.

When I arrived back at the apartment I went in to the bedroom and lay on the bed in a fetal position. I could not cry; there were no tears. I was numb and felt sick.

When the phone rang, it took all my energy just to move off the bed to answer it. My Mom was on the line, and boy was she mad! She started in on me about being stupid. She said that Alfred had bought a set of wedding rings for me and why would I be so stupid as to break up with him? According to my mother, Alfred was a good guy and his family, were "good people." She said that I should get back together with him. I told her that I did not want to get back together with him. Mom was so mad she said "You get what you deserve," and slammed down the phone. I don't remember feeling anything. I was numb. I hung up the phone went back into the bedroom and curled up on the floor in the corner by the bed and stayed there.

That evening Ursula arrived back in Edmonton for school on Monday, and she found me still on the floor. She thought that I was upset and confused about breaking if off with Alfred. She said that I should be happy that someone wanted to marry me and that I should not be such a bitch. I didn't tell her or anyone about being raped, after all they said that I deserved it.

In hindsight, I can see that Alfred had been a very busy little man making everyone feel sorry for him. This would become a pattern that I was going to become all too familiar with.

I finished summer school and arrived back home the middle of August. Now I had to contend with Nelson again and his bitching at me all the time. Since his marriage was over, he had moved in with my parents the year before. He and I never got along, he was such a pain in the ass all the time, bossing me around. *God I thought, in five months I will be finished school and I can move away.* I could not wait to be away from him! All he ever did was lay on the couch feeling sorry for himself.

Man, I hated Nelson, but I could not really understand why. I thought that I was being a bitch and not very sympathetic to his condition. After all he had just lost his wife. But I did not care. I still hated him for some reason. He made me nervous. He would look at me with a strange expression and it gave me the creeps. I did not know why, but there was something that I just could not put my finger on.

What was it? I thought, *Am I crazy? What is wrong with me? God I am so screwed up! No wonder nobody likes me, here I am picking on a guy down on his luck and I have no sympathy for him."*

I felt like Dr. Jekyll and Mr. Hyde, only nobody knew. Every time I looked at him, every time I heard his voice my skin crawled.

> *I have to get it under control, I am being stupid. What is wrong with me? Ted abused me, nobody else.*

Why did I keep having this stupid image of him and me when I was little?

> *I am lying on my brother's bed, my head is at the foot of the bed.*
> *My face is turned right, facing the closet.*
> *My eyes are open but there is no life in them.*
> *Nelson is on top of me, his pants are gone, his penis is erect. His arms are outstretched, he has one hand on each side of my head on the bed. There are cupboards above his head, the cupboards have curtains for doors. The closet has curtains for a door, the door frame to the room has curtains hanging for a door.*
> *The house is quiet. I feel all alone.*

God I must be a sick person to be thinking that he had molested
me, Ted molested me, not Nelson. Oh God, I am a sick person!
Maybe I should get back together with Alfred, after all he says he
loves me. I should be happy that someone wants me.
I am so ugly, I don't feel normal, he deserves better than me.

... leave me alone ...

I had not planned to date when I got home from summer school. I already had my fill of men and did not want to have anything to do with them. Both Jim and Alfred had different plans.

They both had used me in different ways and I knew that I did not want to live my life in third place to a dog, car, boat, etc. in Jim's case, or not be able to talk to anyone for fear of getting the third degree in Alfred's case. I told both of them that I did not want to get serious about anyone. I need some time to figure out my feelings.

I spent the next several months just going out for coffee or a movie or riding my horse. It did not matter where I went, I just wanted to be alone. Most of my friends pressured me to get back together with Alfred and would tell me that I should quit being a bitch and realize that he was a great catch.

What is wrong with me, am I just being selfish? Maybe they're right. I thought.

I needed to prove to myself that the abuse was behind me, that Ted was behind me.

The last year that Jim and I dated, I had a hard time breaking up with him. Jim would always arrive at the farm, crying and wouldn't leave until I saw him.

Since arriving back home from summer school, once again I was feeling trapped. Both Jim and Alfred had started insistently pursuing me, they both still wanted me to go out on dates with them.

Why won't they leave me alone, why won't they just leave me
alone?
I don't want either of them.

Maybe for them it turned in to a contest to see which one would beat out the other. I should have listened to the little voice within me, and taken off. But I was so mixed up about what I was feeling and what everyone was telling me to do.

Do I make everyone else happy or do I make myself happy?

... I give up ...

Several months later, a group of us all crammed into Alfred's car and headed into Grande Prairie to do Christmas shopping. Ursula was buying my Christmas present and did not want me to see it, so I stayed back in the car while everyone else went in to do their shopping. Alfred decided to keep me company.

I told him that he should find someone else to marry him because I would not be able to wear a white wedding dress, my wedding dress would have to be black. He said that he did not care; he still wanted to marry me. I think Alfred figured that I was talking about Jim. I never told him any different. I did not want him to know that I was already ugly and tainted before Jim and I had started going out.

This man still wants me even though I am tainted, maybe I should marry him.
After all, he says he loves me.

On our way home from Grand Prairie, I told Alfred that I had a date with Jim and that he could drop me off at the movie theatre because I was meeting him there. With a slight smile on his face, Alfred informed me that we had passed Jim on our way into to Grande Prairie; he was heading back to town. I thought this was strange that he did not tell me earlier, but dismissed it out of my head. Alfred dropped me off at the theatre and I went in to wait for Jim. A few minutes later Alfred came into the movie theatre and parked his butt in the chair beside me. He told me that he had decided that he wanted to see the same show. I told him that he would have to move when Jim arrived. Jim never showed up. When the show was over Alfred offered me a ride home. Just at that exact moment Jim drove by. He must have thought that Alfred and I had been on a date. I did not hear from him for about two years after that.

Alfred had free range.

Later on, around Christmas time, Alfred and I became engaged. When I told Mom that were we getting married, the first thing she said to me was: "Are you pregnant?"

I thought: *How could she think that?* I thought: *Mom should be happy, after all this is what she wants.*

Why was I always trying to make them proud of me?

The wedding was scheduled for 10 months away. That way no one would be able to say that I was pregnant. Maybe then they would be proud of me.

... warning lights - I think ...

Alfred and I had been engaged for about five months and we had not slept together yet. I finally believed that he loved me for me and not just to have sex with me and dump me.

The first time we made love he called me his "whore." I was horrified. He thought that I was his whore, that I was a whore. I was going to marry this man, and he thought that I was a whore?

I was furious and hurt. I yelled at him "I'm not your whore! I am NOT a whore!"

He said, "I did not mean it the way it sounds, I just popped out like something you say in the heat of passion."

The warming lights were going off all over the place, but I did not trust myself to listen to them.

I felt betrayed and dirty.

Maybe all that stuff with Ted was my fault after all. Maybe I deserved it. Maybe I'm one of those people that ask for it to happen. Oh my God, what is wrong with me? I try to be good, I try to do the right thing but it always comes out wrong.
People must be able to see into my soul and notice that I am bad.

A few days later I was standing in Alfred's bedroom, his closet door was open. I noticed there was a stack about four feet high of Penthouse and Playboy magazines in his closet. I was shocked. I told him that I wanted him to throw them all away. He looked at me and said that he only bought them for the articles. Alfred buried them the following day, and promised that he would never buy them again.

In the many years that followed, that was one of his countless promises that Alfred could not keep.

As the wedding approached, we went through a few ordeals dealing with one of the bridesmaids and what she was to wear. Forgive me, but I was under the assumption that since it was my wedding, then things would be the way that I wanted them. But not according to my mother and Edna, Hank's girlfriend, who was the trouble-making bridesmaid.

My mother had come home from town. I was sitting on the fence beside the house, when she came over to me said "Quit being a bitch, and let Edna wear whatever she wants. If you don't, then Hank won't stand up for Alfred as his best man and you'll have wrecked everything again!"

I looked at Mom, tears welling up in my eyes, and told her "I don't care if they're not in the wedding. Edna is going to wear what everyone else is wearing or not be in the wedding!"

Mom was furious, she turned on her heel and stomped to the house. I got off the fence and walked to the back corral and leaned against the fence. I could not understand why Mom was sticking up for Edna. I knew Hank was her favorite, all of us knew that, but this was my wedding not theirs!

I thought as I was leaning against that fence: *I should have gone to Edmonton and been a stewardess when I had the chance, after all I had the job already. But no, I gave in to all the pressure from everyone and now I am getting married. So now I have to make the most of it. So damn them all, this is my wedding and they will wear what I say!*

CHAPTER SIX

... the dress ...

Your wedding dress is the most beautiful dress that you will ever wear. You are the most beautiful woman in the room, your eyes are shining and the smile on your face is radiant. Today you are pledging your love for someone else and they in turn are pledging their love to you.

I can't say that described me on my wedding day.

My Mom was an excellent seamstress. She made my wedding dress, three bridesmaid's and the two flower girl's dresses. It was a good way to save money. To me, the only thing special about my dress was that Mom made if for me. If my dress was black, I would have had the perfect vampire costume for Halloween.

In town there was a small General Store that carried a little of everything. In the front middle aisle of the store was the sewing center. There you could pick out any pattern you wanted, from baby clothes to wedding dresses. That is where I found the pattern of my "dream dress."

The first pattern that I found was a beautiful gown. It had a high collar that had a heart-shaped opening in the front. The sleeves were long with a fitted bodice and a flare for the bottom part. On the back of the gown was a train that flowed out for about two feet. The collar and upper body and sleeves of the dress were made out of lace, while the bottom was a satin fabric. The woman in the picture was what every bride should look like on her wedding day.

This was the dress. This was my dress. This was my fantasy.

Everyone always said that I was not very good looking and that I was flat-chested and skinny. Hank, Al and my best friend Ursula always called me "flatsy." Ursula always said that I had no shape, and that I was not very attractive to look at. Later, it would take Alfred many years of trying to persuade me that was not true, that it was jealousy talking.

I am sure that Ursula thought that I had it all, a great family, and the freedom to do what I wanted, with guys always asking me out. Ursula and I were complete opposites in body type and shape. I was 5'7" with long legs and weighed 105 pounds, smooth clear complexion, perfectly straight teeth and had silky long brown hair that hung to almost my waist. Oh, and I did have boobs that suited my frame.

While I was standing at the sewing counter looking at the dress pattern, I decided that it would not be my dress. The dress that I actually chose to wear was on the following page of the pattern catalogue: this dress was more fitting for me. It had a high round collar and long sleeves. The bodice was not as fitted and there was only a slight flare at the bottom of the dress. Over the top of the dress was a cape that buttoned up at the chin and hung all the way down to the floor. The completed outfit looked like a cocoon. The only part that you could see of me was my face and hands, the rest was covered up completely with the cape and dress. The dress was the ugliest and plainest thing I had ever seen. That was a fitting dress for me.

I chose this dress because I was so self-conscious of my body and what had happened with Ted. I did not want anyone to see me. I did not want to stand out in the crowd. I did not want anyone looking at me and seeing what Ted had seen or what anyone else had seen. I wanted to fade into the background, become invisible. Besides, I did not deserve to wear the princess dress, because I was not a princess. I was tarnished and ugly and I was lucky to find someone who wanted me.

I picked out the pattern from the cupboard and walked over to the counter and paid for it.

Later on that week, Mom and I headed to Grande Prairie to buy material for the dress and cape. The total cost for the material came to a whopping $30.00. My dress cost less to make then each of the bridesmaid's dresses.

The veil I chose did not cover my face, but it did have three ringlets of ribbon that hung down the back from the crown. Its cost was also $30.00.

I look back at that time and I am furious at how I felt about myself. When I look at the pre-wedding pictures, with me getting dressed, I am saddened at how I thought about myself. In reality, in the photos stood a beautiful young woman getting ready to embark on her new life. I could not see what she thought everyone would see if she allowed them to look deep into her eyes. I was the only one that knew the truth about her and I could not see it anywhere, maybe it was in her eyes but she kept those very closely guarded indeed.

I am angry that two ignorant assholes had the power to destroy that young woman's wedding day.

This was the most important day of her life so far, and there they both stood, one on each of her shoulders whispering to her, telling her that she was worthless and that nobody loved her. That she didn't deserve a nicer dress, that she didn't deserve happiness.

The sub-conscious and the conscious mind is a powerful thing, both sides battling for the right to be heard. But ultimately only one can win the war that rages in her mind, that has ravaged her soul.

How will she continue to survive?
How has she survived so far?
Will this young man love her like he says he does, or will he become like the rest?
Will she ever feel normal, what does normal feel like?
Will she ever know what true love feels like?

To her, that is normal, she has looked in many places to find peace, but hasn't had any luck.

Over the years she has tried being saved twice, and has gone to nearly every church and Sunday school in her town. She talks to God all the time, she has tried to tell her mom about the sexual abuse, she had been on the run for 14 years and has more hiding places than she can count.

Will she continue to look for someone or something to help her? Will she ever find it? Will she ever find peace?

... 1976, my new life ...

I woke up to a cool windy fall day. This was my wedding day.

I had hoped that the leaves would have still been on the trees, but the wind had been making short work of them over the previous few days. Farming always took precedence over anything else, including the date for my wedding. Since I could not get married in May as I had really wanted, then a beautiful fall day with all the fall colors would have be nice. But that did not pan out either.

The wedding was a modest one, and the honeymoon interesting. I have to laugh because I took my small dog Bernie with us. I could not leave him behind. He came with me everywhere I went and the honeymoon was no exception.

Bernie did not like Alfred at all, and during our honeymoon whenever Alfred tied to snuggle up to me in bed, Bernie would attack him. I thought it was funny, but Alfred did not.

Bernie was a small mixed breed dog that stood about 10 inches high. He was jet black with a little bit of white on his chest. I got him when he was 6 weeks old from a girl at school. I was not supposed to have a pet so I told my mom that I found him on the driveway. I said that someone must have dropped him off. I knew if she believed me then I would be able to keep him because there was no one for me to give him back to.

A few days later, Mrs. Jenson outed my story, when Mom told her about my puppy and his peeing in my bedroom on the floor and his crying at night. Mrs. Jensen told Mom that I had gotten the puppy from the daughter of a lady that she worked with at her job. Mom was not too pleased and said that I had to give the puppy back if he continued to whine at night and pee on the floor. Then Mom asked me who was going to look after the puppy when I was in school, for she certainly was not.

So Bernie started to sleep in the bed with me and I would take him out during the night to pee and poo. During the school week, I hid him in the pocket of my shirt or coat, and during recess break and noon hour I would take him out and feed him and let him go to the bathroom. The teachers never caught on that I had Bernie with me every day at school. We became inseparable after that. He was my shadow and would try to bite anyone who he felt was threatening me in any way.

Over the next few years, Alfred and Bernie constantly battled. Alfred did not like Bernie in our bed and would throw him out, but every morning when Alfred got up to get ready for work, he would have to walk a minefield of doggy poo down the hallway that had a blue shag rug.

Bernie would leave small deposits wherever Alfred had to walk, so if the light was not on, guess what? I would hear a lot of swearing and cursing as Alfred wiped off his feet.

The moment Bernie heard the outside door close as Alfred left, he would crawl out from under the bed. He would jump in and curl up beside me, content and happy to be where he belonged.

It was a warm spring morning, and the sun was shining through our bedroom window. Our new mobile home was sitting beside a small dugout. We did not have power or water yet, but that did not matter to me. I was happy. It was better than living in the old 10 foot x 66 foot trailer in Alfred's parents' yard that we had lived in that previous winter. We did not have running water in that trailer either and only half of the electrical plugs worked.

Alfred was already up and had gone over to his parents' house to have his morning coffee. They lived about an eighth of a mile from us. Our new mobile home was set up on a section of their land, just far enough away that his mother could not spy on us. That was her favorite thing to do: watch us from her dining room window. Watching and commenting on everything that I did or did not do right for her son.

When Alfred got back from his coffee he told me that we needed to talk. I asked what the problem was and he said that he was bored with our sex life. We had only been married six months.

I was not sure what to think. My stomach had dropped within me. I sat on the bed and asked if he wanted a divorce.

Once again my mind started to race:

What is wrong with me?
Already this great guy is bored with me, what am I doing wrong?
How can I fix this?
Everyone will think I am defective!

Things from that point on started to get a little uncomfortable for me concerning the bedroom time.

Later that fall we moved to Blue Ridge because Alfred had a transfer from his job. I thought maybe this would be a new beginning, away from his mother and her meddling.

Some days Bernie, Yukon (my Samoyed, who was also very protective) and I would travel with Alfred around on his job checking on oil well sites. It was a boring thing to do, but I loved seeing all the wildlife on our travels. That spring I became pregnant and had our twin daughters in December. It was not an easy time after their birth and I almost died from hemorrhaging. It was three long days in the Grande Prairie hospital before they released me to go to the Blue Ridge hospital where the girls had been born and where they had stayed while I fought for my life.

... meaning ...

My gorgeous twin babies were finally born in the wee hours of Christmas Day. The first baby was a little girl we called Emily. She was perfect, with ten little toes and ten little fingers. She had a bit of long black hair on the crown of her perfectly round head. I have never seen anything so beautiful and perfect. While the nurse was cleaning her off she was making a lot of noise. The head nurse handed her back to me and said, "I think someone is hungry." I nursed Emily before getting ready to deliver the second baby.

I was worn out by the time the second baby decided to appear in the world. The second baby was a bit bigger than the first, so labour had to be started all over again. 45 minutes later, little Tasha appeared in the world. She was perfect and beautiful also with ten little fingers and ten little toes. Her head was covered in soft downy hair. After the nurse cleaned up Tasha I fed her, then when she was done nursing Emily was ready for another feeding.

I took the doctor an hour and half to stitch me up and get me ready to go back to my room. During that time, my legs had started to cramp up from the position they had been in for the past five hours. I was going to be glad to get out of the Delivery Room and into my hospital bed and lay down properly.

I had been in my room for about 2 hours after I had given birth, when I suddenly felt this whooshing feeling in my abdomen. I was not sure what it was but I really had to go to the washroom so I rang the buzzer for the nurse and waited. I was thinking to myself, *WOW, what a Christmas this is, my girls were born on Jesus' birthday!* They were both healthy with ten fingers and ten toes. I could not believe how much I already loved them! I had thought that kind of love was never for me, but I was wrong. My heart was so filled up that I thought it would burst.

When the nurse arrived at my room I told her that I needed to use the washroom. She went to the cabinet and brought out the bedpan and turned to hand it to me. I looked at her and said, "You've got to be kidding! I am not peeing in a bedpan. Could you please help me to the washroom?"

So she attempted to help me to the washroom, but my legs seemed like they didn't want to work properly. I could feel small prickling sensations running up and down them. The next thing I remember, I woke up laying on the floor by my bed with blood everywhere.

There were three doctors and six nurses working above me while I lay helplessly on the floor. They were trying to stop the hemorrhaging, but they were not having any luck. I knew something was wrong. I whispered to them to call Alfred.

I started to think *there's no way in hell I'm going to die now and leave my baby girls behind. I'm going to make sure that what happened to me won't ever happen to them. I'm going to protect them from the Teds of the world. Nobody is ever going to hurt them like that!*

My daughters gave me a reason to fight. I knew that if I could not be normal, I would make sure that they were. They would know what love is. They would not be afraid to go out on dates and to love someone with all their hearts. They would know that I loved them most of all. I vowed that I would hug them every day and tell them that I loved them. I would kiss them goodnight every night and be there every morning when they woke up. My girls would know that their mother would do anything for them. I would listen to them and help them with their problems and not criticize them. They would know that I would walk on broken glass for them and protect them from anyone and anything that would do them harm.

That night I refused to die. That night my baby girls had given me a true purpose to live, my daughters had put meaning back into my soul.

... later, reality sets in ...

I arrived home from the hospital with the twins on New Year's Eve. Alfred and I still had not opened our Christmas present to each other.

That year for Christmas, I was given two beautiful daughters and a whole lot of lingerie, the latter being something that I was not in the mood for.

A few weeks before the girls were born, Mom had said that she would come and help me after I got out of the hospital. She never came. I had been home for a few days when I phoned her and asked when she was coming. She said she was too busy at home. At that time I could have sure used the help. My mother-in-law came instead for one week. I was very grateful for the help that she had provided during that week.

I could not believe that my own mother would not help me after I had almost died! My body was having a hard time adjusting to the more than nine units of new blood and plasma that had been pumped into me. I was craving things that I had never eaten or drank before. I was weak and my hands were constantly cracking from touching the wet diapers. All of these symptoms lasted for about three months until my own blood replaced the blood from the donors.

During this time, things changed drastically for Alfred and me.

I did not have time to devote to Alfred, as the babies were a constant demand on my time. Alfred refused to get up at night and help me with the girls. He said it gave him a headache to wake up in the middle of the night. If he was forced to get up in the night because I was too exhausted, then I had three babies to deal with the next day or two, as his headache would prevent him from going to work. The girls woke up every three hours. They never slept through the night until they were about two years old.

Within five months of the girls' birth we had moved to High Level, about five hours from our families. This move was supposed to provide Alfred with electrical training and advancement, but in reality what it did provide was a way for him to be away from home for three weeks at a time. I was stuck over 500 hundred miles from anyone that might have helped me with the girls. I was on a dead run from sun up to sun down and in between, as the girls did not sleep through the night yet. The only peace that I would get is when the girls would lay on floor on a blanket, kicking their legs and trying to roll over. Bernie would lay beside them on the blanket, guarding them and Yukon would lay by the front door, watching. If the babies moved too far off the blanket then Bernie would yip at me to come and organize them again back on the blanket. Soon the twins were moving and rolling all over the place, so then I put each of them in small walkers with pillows supporting their backs. The girls soon learned to push with one foot to move the walker and followed me around the trailer while I cleaned.

The decision to move back to our hometown was made two months later when Alfred came home one weekend and the girls made strange to him. Our mobile home, that we had bought a few years before, was moved into town and the girls and I moved home. Alfred was out of a job as the company had told him that if he moved they would have to fire him, even though all the work that he had been doing for them was in fact in our hometown. That did not matter, they had moved him to High Level at their expense, and he was supposed to stay there for two or more years until someone else decided that they want to replace him. The last guy had lived there for over 10 years.

Life at home became less hectic and within the next few years, Alfred's new passion started to grow. Soon the varieties of

Penthouse, Playboy and S&M magazines started to show up, and the desires that he read about and pictures that he looked at started to plant seeds and grow.

I could not understand why I was not enough. I was now sharing our intimate life with all those girls in the magazines and Alfred had disgusting and scary ideas of what I should be doing for him and how. There was no way in hell I was ever going to do those things that were pictured in the magazines.

I thought: *Who and what are you? This was not what I had signed up for. I thought you were a safe choice.*

Boy, was I starting to learn the error in that judgment.

Life for me once again became a struggle for survival, and a struggle for my own existence, but now I had nowhere to run and hide. I now had two babies that needed me. And I needed them.

CHAPTER SEVEN

... trust no one with your children ...

We had been back living in our hometown for about one year, and the girls were almost two years old. I had several appointments that day and needed someone to watch the girls for me. My mom was busy, as was "Wheezy" (a private nickname given to my miserable chain-smoking mother-in-law), so I asked my sister-in-law, Ursula if she could watch them for me. She said, "Sure no problem."

I said, "I don't want Edna watching them, only you." Edna was my other sister-in-law.

Ursula said, "I understand, she won't be here."

"Good," I replied

Both Al and Ursula, and Hank and Edna lived in trailers beside each other on my father's property. The trailers were set up on the east side of the trees that lined the east side of my parents' yard. Both Hank and Al were helping with the farming, so dad figured it would be a good idea if they lived on the property. Edna had been such a pain in my ass before the wedding, and during the wedding and she continued to be one after. I did not trust her with the girls' welfare.

I dropped the girls off with Ursula. She and Al had a couple of little kids for the girls to play with. I figured that they would have fun playing all day until I got back to pick them up.

When I arrived about six hours later to get the girls, I went to Ursula's trailer and knocked on the door but there was no answer. My stomach suddenly did a flip flop, I drew in a long breath and then I walked over to Edna and Hanks' trailer and knocked on the door. The minute the girls saw me they came running out crying and grabbed my legs. I bent down to ask them what the matter was. That is when I noticed that their eyes were extremely red and swollen. They looked like someone had been beating them. I was horrified and turned and asked Ursula, "What happened to them?"

Ursula said, "Oh, nothing they had a fight with the other kids and started crying just before you got here."

I said, "It looks like they've been crying for a while."

She shrugged her shoulders. I was not impressed.

I wanted to ask Ursula "Why in the hell were the girls at Edna's place after I told you not to let Edna near them?" but I knew that was pointless. Whatever had happened was already done. I just was not sure what that was. I gently asked the girls what had happened but they just shook their little heads, no. They were not ready to tell me anything at that moment.
A few days later, the girls and I were in town picking up groceries when I ran into Ursula and Edna. The instant the girls saw them they jumped behind me and hung onto my legs. The girls were shaking so badly, I thought they were going to pull my jeans off. I glared at Ursula and Edna and with as much calm as I could muster I asked, "What happened at your house the other day?"

Both of them, stared at the girls then at me and said at the same time, "Nothing."

I continued to glare at them and replied, "Well someone is going to tell me what happened or there will be hell to pay."

Then I turned and with the girls clutching each of my legs walked to my car.

Later that night I called Ursula to find out what happened. She told me that Edna had come over and did not want the girls playing with her kid so she locked them in the bedroom all day without food or water. She said that their little hands were sticking out from under the door begging and crying to be let out.

I was sick to my stomach with what I just heard.

Ursula said that she did not want to cause a fight so she never said anything to Edna or tried to stop her.

I hung up the phone and phoned Edna right away and asked her what happened, she told me the same story but inserted Ursula's name in the story instead of her own.

The next day I paid a surprise visit to them both, I told them that I held both of them responsible for abusing the girls and that they were the most despicable sick twisted bitches I had ever met. I asked them "What kind of mothers are you to pick on two innocent little girls? I told them, "If you have a problem with me, then take it out on me and not them. You are both cowards!"

When I told Mom what had happened to the girls while Ursula was watching them, she did not believe me. Mom refused to believe that Edna (her favorite son's wife) could do something so wrong, and as for Ursula, why would she do it? I stressed to mom that if she was watching the girls for me that the girls were not allowed to go over to Edna's or Ursula's place. I stressed that if she could not do that, then the girls could not come to the farm any more.

I found out much later that Mom did not heed my concern regarding Edna and Ursula.

It was years before the girls would approach either Edna or Ursula.

I was so mad at myself for letting the girls down, I had promised to protect them from abuse and I had failed. I hoped that they would not carry those scars for the rest of their lives. I talked to them about why some people do bad things to other people and that it was not their fault that their aunties were not very nice people. I told them that I loved them very much and I would not let Ursula and Edna hurt them ever again.

... Wheezy, the "Hell" woman ...

In March of 1981 we sold our mobile home and with Dad's help, and we bought an old house that needed to be moved off a lot in town. Alfred's parents, Stan and Wheezy, wanted us to move back onto their property so that they could be near the girls. I was not so sure, but they insisted and said that the property would be willed to Alfred after their death, so we may as well live there now.

Allowing Alfred to convince me to move us there would turn out to be one of the biggest mistakes of my life. Living in the same yard with my mother-in-law again was driving me crazy. Over the following years I continued to suggest to Alfred that we should move to our own place, but he refused saying, "We could not afford it and besides Mom and Dad said we could buy their place."

I replied, "When is that going to happen?"

Alfred said "They want to sell it to us for $12,000 with the option that they can remain living there until they die or move off."

I thought for a minute and said, "I want it in writing and not a verbal agreement."

Funny thing is, all of a sudden things changed with Alfred. He refused to ask them. He said that a verbal agreement for him was good enough. I am not sure if this was in fact a true agreement or one that Alfred had made to shut me up about getting our own place away from his mother.

So the abuse from his mother continued. She constantly would yell at me from her porch whenever she saw me outside. She screamed all kinds of abuse on any given day. She would scream that I was not good enough for her son, that I was a terrible mother, that I cared about the horses more than the girls, that I was selfish, that I was useless. The list went on and on.

Once again, my health had been slowly deteriorating. All of the stress from Alfred and his mother was starting to cause me to have severe abdominal pain. The pain would strike after one her screaming attacks. Alfred did not like it if I screamed back at her to mind her own business and to go back into her house and leave me alone. Alfred would say that he did not agree with his mother but he could not stop her so I should just ignore her. I thought to myself: *Are you frigging kidding me, you spineless wimp?*

I was in the yard one summer day. Wheezy had just finished tying into me again about my care or lack of care of the girls. She stood on her deck, smoking her cigarette, puffing out her chest, glaring at me. I just could not understand what her problem was. I had never done anything to the old bitch. I turned to go back to our house to check on the girls, who were playing on our lawn. I hoped that they did not hear their grandmother. All of a sudden my stomach cramped so badly that I collapsed on the ground. I could not move. Sweat was starting to run down my face and I was feeling cold and clammy.

Alfred was puttering around with his tools in the tool shed we had beside our house, when he heard his mother screaming at me again. He did not come out of the shed to confront his mom, instead he ignored her.

When he heard me gasp and fall to the ground he came running over to me to see what the problem was. He must have gotten scared because he yelled at his mother to watch the girls because he was taking me to the hospital.

Wheezy just stood there glaring with a smirk on her face puffing on her cigarette.

Alfred managed to get me into the vehicle and away we went to the emergency room in our local hospital. I could barely walk from the car to the hospital doors without wanting to fall down. I had made it past the inside sliding doors when I collapsed on the floor in the lobby. The nurses ran over with a wheelchair and started to ask me questions. When the doctor arrived, he asked me where it hurt and what had brought on the stomach pains. I managed to tell him that my mother-in-law was screaming at me in the yard, and that she was calling me names and telling me that I was a terrible mother. The doctor looked at me, then asked "How long has this being going on?"

I replied, "Ever since I married her son, about 10 years ago."

He prescribed "Stress Tabs."

These episodes became an increasing familiar scene over the next few years. Wheezy stalked me constantly. She would sit at her dining room window watching for me to come out from our house. Then she would attack. She could see into our side family room window from her dining room and she could also see the back and front doors of our house. I soon started to go outside from our laundry room door on the other side of the house, but the minute she saw me in the yard the attacks would start.

It did not matter what old Wheezy said to me, Alfred never told her any different. He never told her to mind her own business. He never told her that she was wrong, he just told me to ignore her. I think the only person that stood up to Wheezy was her husband Stan.

It was a nice and warm day out, a perfect day for the girls and me to go for a ride on the horses. We headed to the corrals to catch the three horses Red, Domino and Baer.

Red was Emily's pony. He was chestnut gelding that stood about 13.2 hh (hands high). Domino was a pinto pony standing about 14.2 hh and Baer was my black anglo-arab gelding that stood about

16 hands. I had just finished helping the girls put on their tack and now was getting Baer ready to be saddled.

I heard Wheezy's screen door open and close. I took a deep breath and braced myself for the attack. Thank heavens the girls had ridden their ponies to the back of the yard, past the trees. I was hoping that they were not going to hear their grandmother again.
As she was yelling at me about what a low-life I was, I stood there on the other side of Baer, breathing in his scent, focusing on trying to stay calm in all the turmoil. My legs were starting to shake again and I had to hang onto Baer's mane to stop me from falling to the ground. I refused to give her that satisfaction after the last time I collapsed and ended up in the emergency room at our local hospital.

Stan and Wheezy had been married right after her first divorce, and Alfred was his only son. I am not sure how he stayed married to her.

Stan and I got along really well. He would help me fix the fences for the horses, build their shelters and haul hay for them. Everyone that knew our family would always say that Stan and I acted more like we were married than Alfred and I. If I made some different kind of dessert or even French toast, Stan would say that it was delicious and maybe Wheezy should get the recipe. That would really piss her off.

Maybe he did it to get back at her for something, or maybe he just liked his daughter-in-law, I am not sure. But that day he told Wheezy to leave me alone and to go back into their house. Amazingly she did.

I had ended up in the emergency room a few more times after that, but on my last visit the doctors consulted together and told me that I was suffering from anxiety. They said if I ever needed to talk about what was happening, to call the doctor's office and book into the last appointment of the day.

I never went back to the hospital after that last attack. I knew that there was nothing they could do for me. I was not going to let my nervous breakdown become common knowledge in the small town. I refused to give Wheezy one more thing to bitch at me about or to use against me to take the girls away from me. I had heard rumors that she wanted me gone from their son's life and that she wanted evidence to support that I was not stable, then she would finally be able to force me to leave.

She did get part of her wish the following year in 1986. Alfred had finally gotten a job after 4 years of nothing. I was tired from working three jobs at the same time, trying to keep food on the table and the bills paid.

Alfred's new job entitled him to be away from home for 8 days at a time and then at home for six days. He was going to be working in the oilfield and living in a camp about 150 miles into the bush.

… little things …

It was the end of August when Alfred finally left for his first shift out at the camp, I thought that I was in heaven, but my heaven would soon come to a crashing halt.

The damage to our marriage was still there, and within a few months Alfred and I separated for the first time. He moved in with his parents across the yard and the girls and I stayed in the house. Alfred had full access to our house and to me, unfortunately, when he was home from work. He took this time to start his "pity me game." Alfred would bring over sad love songs about the woman leaving their man and the dog dying. When these songs didn't work, he would then take off his wedding band and ask me to hold it for him so that it would mend his broken heart when he put it back on. This behaviour went on for months.

When Alfred headed back to camp after his six days off, then his mother would start in on me. After months of Wheezy's nagging, Alfred's constant calling on the phone and his sister voicing angry insults to me, I could not take it anymore and gave in and let him move back in.

I remember wishing that I had someone to turn to and help me "get out of Dodge." No one knew what was going on, and I knew that no one would believe me even if I told them. After all, this was Alfred, everybody's friend. Everyone liked Alfred. It felt like I was trapped and forced to live the rest of my life like that and I had resigned myself to the fact.

Over the next few years, little things started to get stuck in my mind. I knew that Alfred was fooling around with someone else, but every time I questioned him he denied it. Without proof I did not have a leg to stand on.

Your sixth sense or intuition does not count. Sometimes, you need proof.

Alfred soon started talking about the young female cook that was on his shift at the camp. When he was at home on his days off, she would always phone him. One time he told me that when he went to her house to pick her up for their shift, she opened the door with no clothes on. I asked him what did he do and he said that he turned around and left. I did not believe him.

I knew for sure that he had lied when we headed off to Edmonton for the weekend with the girls. We were in West Edmonton Mall sitting down on a bench beside the ice rink when all of a sudden here was the young camp cook and her husband. I looked at her and then to Alfred, but before I could say anything he cut in and said to the camp cook, "Wow, fancy meeting you guys here, what a coincidence."

I heard that a few months later she was fired for having sexual relations with someone while at camp. This was a dry camp (no alcohol) and was promoted as a non-sexual environment between employees while at camp.

Rumors and stories travel fast in a work environment and the big boys in head office had noticed Alfred's little part time activity with the camp cook. Alfred was now being watched by his bosses.

Soon Alfred started to slip into Edmonton from the camp, he would be gone for hours at a time. I would phone him on his truck phone to see how his day was going but could never reach him, so then I would call the office to talk to him but I was told he was not there either. When I could not reach him and his boss could not reach him, rumors started up again. Things were about to get sticky for Alfred and for our family.

With all these little things adding up I finally asked him again if he was fooling around. Again he would deny it and would tell me that I was the only woman he loved.

I do believe that I am the only woman he actually did love. In Alfred's mind he was not cheating on me because he did not love his other partners. I also thought that it was strange that Alfred thought that claiming that he loved me, but having sex with multiple partners, was not wrong.

I wondered where Alfred learned that line of thinking. Was it from all his dirty little sex magazines that he enjoyed so much or was he just demented in the head?

Over the years I had found that it was easier for me to try and keep him on an even keel than it was to argue with him about activities that he constantly denied. Alfred had a knack for making my life hell if he did not get his way or if he felt that I did not love him the way he thought I should. When he was mad and out of control he would throw and smash things in the house or his vehicle, or get drunk and sometimes even disappear for days at a time. But when he was angry and in better control of himself, then the air in the house turned to ice. It was easier to keep him happy and never make any comments about him or what he did.

... the tote bag ...

Over the years Alfred had secretly continued to buy bondage magazines and hide them in the basement of our house.

Things boiled up for me one day when I went downstairs to check on the girls playing in their playroom. Both of the girls were sitting on the floor with a bondage magazine opened in their laps. I was mortified! I quickly took the magazines away from the girls and asked them where they found them. They went over to Alfred's work cabinet and opened the door. There, piled in the bottom of the cabinet, were hundreds of these magazines depicting women in very degrading positions, with ropes around their necks or their hands and legs bound. Some pictures had women stretched and hanging like a piece of meat while other photos were with ropes cutting through their genital area.

It was gross. I could not understand what his obvious desire to view such grotesque pictures was. I suddenly had a very sickening feeling and thought, *Is this what I'm in store for, does he want me to be like the women in his magazines?* I felt a chill run down my spine.

It was not long after that I discovered the "tote bag" of his goodies. I had assumed that the duffel bag was his dirty work clothes from camp. Boy, was I surprised when I unzipped it.

In the tote bag was a collection of various weird sex toys that Alfred had bought, and some that he had made himself. He apparently took great pride in this bag and had spent many hours perfecting his tools. There were different types of ropes with various sizes of loops, some to fit my hands and feet and some to apparently fit his. There were teat pinchers, ball squeezers, penis things, leather whips, and thick one inch chains both long and short lengths, horse hobbles, vibrators, butt plugs and more. There were even certain types of lingerie and stilettos, too big for me.

Alfred was obsessed with sex, stories about sex, and clothes for sex, anything to do with sex. I felt that I had married a monster, a sexual deviant. I did not know who he was anymore. Maybe I never did know him after all.

How well do you ever really know someone and their secrets?

Alfred started to press me hard to participate with him in his sex games. When I refused, he would tell me that if I truly loved him then I would do as he asked. I was forced to cave in a little bit at a time. I hated it, and I hated myself for being so weak.

Finally I could not take it anymore and I told him to get out and go live with his parents.

I was moving on with my life and with the girls. About two months later, I met a nice man named Terry. He was from Texas and was working in the area for a time. We hit it off.

Alfred was furious and he enlisted his best friend and wife, to help watch my every move when I was in town or at work. She worked at the same place I did. Edna reported to Alfred everyday what she knew about my comings and goings.

One winter weekend, I took the Greyhound bus to visit Terry in the nearby area that he was working at. I was on my way back home on the Greyhound bus when it suddenly pulled over to the side of the highway. Everyone was looking around to see what the problem was. One of the passengers asked the bus driver what was going on, he replied that there was a car in front of him forcing him to stop. When the bus had come to a complete stop, the driver opened the door, Alfred boarded the bus and dragged me off by my hair. Nobody on the bus moved to stop him.

I am amazed that the bus driver did not stop him, I guess that he was afraid of him. At that moment I knew that I sure was, but I refused to let him see the look on my face. Thank God it was dark outside. After he shoved me into the car we started to drive away. You could cut the tension in the car with a knife. I was getting worried that something had happened to the girls, but I needed to diffuse the tension in the car first, so I calmly asked him if anything had happened at home.

He never answered, so then I asked him if the girls were okay. When he said the girls were fine, I breathed a sigh of relief.

Now my fear was turning into anger and I turned and asked him "What in the in hell do you think you are doing? If this is how you are trying to mend our marriage you sure have a lot to learn! I am not changing my mind."

We drove in silence for the next hour until we got back to our house. I went into my house and he went over to his parents. If he thought that he was coming in with me, then he was sadly mistaken again.

The next day he sent over the "big gun": his mother. She walked right into my house uninvited. Wheezy told me that I could leave and move to Texas, but over her dead body was I going to take the girls with me. With her beady cold eyes staring at me she said "The girls will live with me and I will make sure that you lose custody of them. You will never see them ever again! They will be better off with me than you. All you care about is your stupid horses. You are selfish and worthless. My son will be better off without you!"

I stood there in my bathroom, not really surprised by her and her sick ideas. I looked back at her with as much disgust as I could afford I replied, "I am not going anywhere, I am not moving to Texas, and you will not be looking after the girls, they already have a mother, whether you like it or not."

I am not sure why she thought that I would be moving to Texas. I assumed it was Alfred who told her I was. I knew that I had to be careful how I dealt with Alfred's bitch of a mother, I knew that he would never stand up to her for me regarding the girls' welfare, and I knew, financially, I still had to live in this yard with her and her constant meddling.

I had heard the rumors that Wheezy had a reputation for lying. I was told that she had gone to court with her daughter because of child custody battles and lied about things regarding the children's care from their fathers.

I could not give Wheezy the chance to get my girls. I held my ground for three more months, then finally had to give in again and stayed in the marriage. But I counted the days until I could leave forever.

I find that writing about parts of my life with Alfred and Wheezy is very taxing on my mental self. The feeling of complete desperation still engulfs me as I edit the stories trying to say exactly how I felt and how everything affected my way of thinking. I don't think that I will ever be able to describe the feeling of having someone always telling you that you are not good enough, or someone trying to force you to do things that you can't in the name of what he calls love.

I know that if the abuse with Ted and Nelson had not happened, I would never have married Alfred. I would not have been looking for someone that I initially perceived as safe.

I can say that the one silver lining through all of this is that if I did not marry Alfred, I would not have my girls. I would marry Alfred again and again if it meant getting my girls.

... the nightmare ...

We had been living back in Alfred's parents' yard for about two years, when I started to have nightmares about a grizzly bear. I would wake up in the middle of the night from this recurring nightmare of a grizzly bear trying to crawl through our family room window to eat me. I would be shaking all over with sweat running down my back. Every time, for some reason, I would have the need to go to the washroom and there was no waiting until morning. So I would slip out of bed and crawl on my hands and knees around the end of the bed to the door of our bedroom, then almost crawl on my belly to the bathroom beside our bedroom and slip in. Once in the bathroom I could turn on the light, the bear could not see me in the bathroom. It took some time for me to calm down enough to walk out of the bathroom and back into our bedroom to go to bed.

When I looked out of our bedroom door I could see the family room window about eight feet beside me. It was 5 feet wide and 6 feet tall. Our house was in the shape of an "L," facing west was our living room and family room and our bedroom. The living room and family room windows were very large. On the south side was our bedroom window, then the bathroom was opposite the dining room. An addition that had been added contained the kitchen, laundry room, office, porch area and stairs to the basement.

The grizzly bear nightmare never quit happening until I left for good in 1996.

Years later, I finally looked up what the dream meant and found out that if you have an aggressive and overbearing person in your life you will dream about bears. I thought to myself, *I sure did have that with old Wheezy.*

... broken trust ...

After discovering Alfred's latest pastime regarding woman's clothes, peep shows in Edmonton, and 1-888 sex hot lines, I only had to wait for the next two years to go by before I could leave for good. At the end of those two years the girls would have graduated from high school and be 18 years old or close to it depending on when I got a new job and wherever I was going to end up living.

One afternoon I was putting away Alfred's laundry in his top drawer when my hand brushed against a paper bag near the bottom of his underwear. I pulled out the package and opened it. It was a sexy red lacy top and bikini bottom, in a large size.

For nineteen years Alfred had been buying me lingerie and in those 19 years he never had gotten the size wrong. I thought to myself that he was going to have to come up something better than, "I made a mistake in the sizing."

Alfred was outside helping his dad put in a fence post by the corral. I stood on the deck watching him....thinking that I finally had proof of his cheating.

When Alfred came into the house, I stood at the counter in the kitchen looking at him. He looked at me and asked what the problem was.

I looked back at him with a benign look on my face and said, "In two years, as soon as the girls graduate I am leaving."

I don't think he took me seriously, after all that was two years away and he could do a lot of persuading in that time.

When I confronted with the sexy red lingerie, his comment was, "Oh, I made a mistake in the size."

For the next two years, I never mentioned the hidden phone bills with the sex calls he made during the wee hours of the night wherever I was away riding in Camrose on weekends, or the extra-large lingerie and stilettos or the tote bag. I never made a comment about his losing his job because of his sexual escapades to Edmonton on company time, and once again not finding work to support his family. I never mentioned anything. I just waited, and pretty soon he thought he was safe.

Two more years was not a long time to wait for my freedom from him. I now started to make plans as to how I was going to get away from him with my life. I knew after the last time I left him that he would sooner kill me than let me leave freely.

CHAPTER EIGHT

... the beginning of a new life ...

It was finally time to leave the marriage for good. I no longer had to worry about custody of the girls. I was not sure how everyone was going to take the news that I was leaving, so I decided to talk to the girls first about me leaving, and then tell my father. If the girls objected, then I would have to stay, no matter how I felt about it, to me their welfare and happiness came first.

It was the beginning of summer of 1996 when I told the girls that I wanted to talk to them about something. The three of us went for a short walk to the creek behind our house. I figured that I would tell them where it was peaceful and calm.

I had agonized over how I would tell them that I was leaving in a few months and decided that the best way was to tell them part of the truth. I told the girls that I was going to leave their father, and that we would be getting a divorce. I asked them if they would have a problem with it. I was amazed when their reply was "Fine, it is not like Dad does anything around here. It's always you and Grandpa that do everything. Dad is always fishing or hunting."

I was not sure what to think with that response, but I told them that I would be moving and I wanted them to come with me. They said that they wanted to stay where their friends were. Then they asked me if they were going to be living in the house alone. I told them that they would still be living in the house if I moved away.

I think they were more interested in the fact that they would be living on their own, without parents. Alfred was now living in Red Deer and was never at the house anyway. Since he was self-employed with his own Oilfield Company, he had chosen to get an apartment close to the job he was hired to oversee. With no bosses to watch him, he now had total freedom and the time to devote to his obsession without me there.

The next step for me was to tell my dad that I was leaving Alfred.

I needed to know if Dad would be disappointed in me for giving up on the marriage. All I have ever wanted since I was a kid was to make my dad proud of me. He was the only one in my family that stood up to Mom when she wanted to put me in foster care.

Again I was surprised with his response when I told him the news.

Dad said, "Sis, I will stand behind you in anything that you decide to do. I have seen you work three jobs at once while Alfred sat at home on his ass. Your mother and I have never interfered with your life, but it is about time you left him."

Now that the girls and my dad knew, the next steps in my plan were: to find a new job; to find someplace to board my eight horses, and to get Alfred to think it was his idea for me to move away.

We may have been living in separate houses at the time, but I knew that I was Alfred's possession and he would not give that up easily. His living somewhere else was only to provide him with time and desire to follow his passions without my knowledge.

... moving on alone ...

It was October 1996 and time to move. My three competition horses had already been moved to a stable outside of Camrose, now it was my turn to load up what stuff that I had gathered for furniture and such. The girls still did not want to move and most of the furniture and dishes were staying in the house for them to use.

With a few suggestions from me over the summer months about the cost of traveling back and forth riding, Alfred had decided that it would be more practical if I lived near where the horses were being trained instead of driving the seven hours one way every weekend to train them. I knew from past experience that I could not really tell him that I was leaving, even though I made it very clear two years before that it was happening. I knew that I had to put some distance between us before asking for the divorce. I also knew that I needed to have a place of my own and a job so that he could not drag me back. I had to be self-sufficient in every way possible.

After I had settled into the new apartment, I went back home to visit the girls. The girls and I talked on the phone everyday about four to five times a day, I missed them as much as they missed me. The girls decided that they wanted to see where I was living, so the next weekend the girls hopped on the Greyhound bus and came to Camrose for the weekend.

I had hopes that they would love it there and want to move also, but that did not happen. The girls were looking forward to living on their own, and had no intention of moving with me.

For the next seven months I worked and trained the horses. Living on my own was suiting me well. Every once in a while Alfred would show up, but I could handle that. Soon, every time he came to the apartment he would look around, like he was looking for something, but I was not sure what that something was.

I was starting to get nervous about his frequent visits. One particular summer day, Alfred stopped in. He was sitting at the kitchen table looking at me while I was standing at the counter looking back. He said," I am going to move in here with you."

The blood drained from my face. I asked, "Why?"

"Because I want to and we can save money," was his reply.

I remember standing there thinking to myself: *there is no way in hell you are going to move in here.*

Unfortunately for me, when I get really nervous and a confrontation is about to happen, my lips start to quiver and it looks like I am smirking. This did not look good for me, so I quickly replied back, "I want a divorce."

Alfred was not surprised by this, all he said was, "Fine, but you can't see anyone else and we'll still have sex when I want it from you."

I stood my ground and said, "You can't tell me who I can or cannot see, we are getting a divorce. As for sleeping with you, that is not going to ever happen again. Divorce means just that. Done. Finished. "

He got really angry. He jumped up out of the kitchen chair and stormed towards the door, then he swung around and said," There are five things that I am going to do to you before this is done.

> One: I will ruin your relationship with the girls;
> Two: I will ruin you financially;
> Three: I will have you fired from your job;
> Four: you will have no friends and family when I am done with you; and

Five: You WILL come crawling back to me!"

He opened the door and walked out, slamming to door so hard that the cupboards shook.

I was still standing by the counter, unable to move, holding my breath, shaking inside. My mind was racing, *Wow, I finally did it, I am going to be free.*

The only thing that saved me during that time was Bud. I had met Bud a few years before this at a training seminar for life insurance. He was the facilitator teaching the course in Grande Prairie.

When I had left Alfred I was working in a general insurance office in a neighboring town. Alfred knew where the office was and when I was working, he had free access to me five days a week and I could not escape from him.

The Life Insurance company that Bud was working for had put in a new pilot program to recruit new agents to work for them. The program provided new agents with on-the-job training, a steady income and a vehicle with traveling expenses. Bud knew that I had my Life, Accident and Sickness insurance license, so he contacted me and told me about the new program. Bud was the field trainer for the new agents, and helped the new agents to form a strong relationship with the agencies that the company had provided for us.

This was my chance. Alfred would not know where I worked now. He would not be able to find me.

The next two years were a living hell. Alfred broke into my apartment and stole my work day timer and registration papers for the horses, so that I could not sell them. He stalked me whenever I was out of town working. This was easy, since my schedule was in that day timer. He called constantly on my work cell phone telling me that he was going to shoot me because he knew where I was. He said that he had the gun pointing at the motel door, and the minute I opened it "Bam, you're dead!"

Bud, and the change to the new job saved my life.

The following fall, during one of our sessions at the lawyers, Alfred was acting crazy, screaming at his lawyer and my lawyer, throwing things and acting wild. My lawyer had me sit in another room and told me not to come out until after Alfred was gone.

Bud had been sitting in his car outside waiting for me. He drove me to the lawyers as I was a nervous wreck having to meet Alfred again.

When Alfred had finally left the office, and when I did not come out of the lawyer's office, Bud came in. Before Bud could find me, my lawyer took him aside and said, "Don't let her out of your sight, he will kill her!"

Bud took that warning to heart and from that day forward he stayed near me as much as he could, whenever I was not running on the road staying one step ahead of Alfred while I worked.

I lived on the run for two years. I have given up my apartment in Camrose and lived in my company car and stayed in hotel rooms whenever I worked out of town, and that turned out to be most of the time. I had elected to take a big territory so I could be on the road seeing clients.

During the winter months, I would stay in Grande Prairie where Bud had moved to. Bud left the insurance business after his separation and divorce. He needed to get his life back together and had had success in Grande Prairie selling cars. Over the past years, he had lost the connection with his three children from his first marriage, and now also the children that he had raised in his second marriage due to the divorce.

Between Alfred and his parents, they succeeded for a long time in turning my girls against me. They constantly told the girls that I was seeing multiple men and sleeping around. They said that Bud and I were having an affair, and that is why I left Alfred. He preached to the girls constantly that he was so devastated by my actions that he was going to kill himself.

This was so hard on the girls, they did not want to be involved in this mess, but they could not escape. They had become his and his parents' weapons. Alfred and his parents did not care how this was affecting the girls, they only wanted vengeance, and it did not matter who was in the way or who they used. Both the girls became very bitter and pulled into themselves for survival. It became very bad for the girls if Alfred and his parents found out that they talked to me or if they were seen with me. So it was easier for them not to have a relationship with me.

Alfred's Threat Number One = Success.

Alfred stole all the money that I had in my bank account. Still to this day I don't know how he managed that one, but he did. Over the next two years, Alfred did everything in his power to ruin me financially. Finally he succeeded, and I was forced to sell my prized horse Arion in order to keep him safe from Alfred's obsession to constantly try and find Arion and shoot him. I eventually could no longer afford to board Arion anywhere, or to ensure his safety.

Alfred's Threat Number Two = Success

Alfred would call all of our friends that we had had while married and tell them his side of the divorce story. It is true about the old saying, "In a divorce you find out who your true friends are." Then he conspired with Hank and Edna to call him whenever I went to the farm to visit my parents. The minute I arrived, they would call him and tell Alfred what I was wearing and what I was doing. Then he would call my cell number and when I answered he would say that he had me in his sights of his gun, then he would tell me what I was wearing. I was terrified and soon quit going to the farm.

Alfred's Threat Number Four = Partial Success

I was afraid to tell anyone where I was staying or where I was at. The only contact the girls had for me was my work cell phone, the same for my parents. Alfred even went so far as to break into my parents' home one winter while they were in B.C. to see if he could find my address. We found that out after his death when we had to clean up his affairs. Alfred had receipts from my parents in his possession along with night vision goggles.

The minute that Alfred found out that I had a new job, he started to call my new boss and tell him that I was using company expense money to screw Bud while out of town. Thank God, my new boss had known Bud for years and knew the story about the divorce (because I had told him during the interview and said that Alfred would be calling him) so he paid no attention to his ranting. When that did not work, he then phoned the Head Office and complained to the National Sales Manager that I was using company money to screw around with Bud. The following month, after that phone call, the National Sales Manager came to Edmonton and I had to prove that all of my expenses while on the road were indeed acquired while doing business.

Alfred's Threat Number Three = Failed

As for Number Five: There was no way in hell that I was ever going to crawl back to that bastard. If I could survive my childhood and teen years, I surely could survive him.

Number Five = FAILED!

Also during this time Alfred was looking to see where I had all of my horses stashed. He called me constantly, telling me that he was going to shoot them. The three competition horses I had at the barn were moved to the new wing of stalls. Thank heavens, because sure enough Alfred headed to the stable to shoot them all but could not find them where he had last seem them stabled. My trainer had caught wind of him coming there and moved my horse trailer and the horses to safety. The other five horse were staying at a friend's farm near Bashaw. He also worked in the insurance field and had offered to help me.

During the divorce discoveries Alfred's lawyer was constantly trying to pressure me into telling her where the horses were. Alfred's and his lawyer's new tactic was that they needed proof that the horses were being looked after since they were matrimonial property. I refused to tell them. When that did not work, then they would badger me for my address. I also refused to say where I was living. They did not need to know that I was living in my horse trailer during the warmer weather. No one knew except Bud where I was living or not living.

The pressure and the stress of everything soon started to take its toll on me and I started to suffer from anxiety attacks that would cripple me. During these attacks I would shrink into my head and would not come back out. I felt at peace there, floating in the air, weightless with no worries, no cares. No one could reach me there, I was safe.

Poor Bud, he was beside himself when these attacks happened, and they happened usually after a disturbing conflict with my girls regarding the stories that their father was telling them. My girls meant the world to me and I was powerless to help them cope with the divorce. They did not want my advice or counsel on anything. Alfred and his mother had made sure that I had no credibility with the girls.

All during the separation and divorce, Alfred constantly sent me lingerie, horse magazines and pieces of jewellery and very long letters, telling me how much he loved me and missed me. He would send these little packages via the Greyhound bus to whatever town I was at. All the bus depot staff had to do was call my cell phone and tell me that I had a package there. Not knowing who it was from, the girls or my parents, I would have to go and pick it up.

It never stopped. I was afraid to tell anyone where I was staying or where I was at for fear of Alfred showing up or his little packages. I think he had many spies working for him.

After the breakup of our marriage, Alfred did not have to worry that I would catch on to his schemes, so he dove deeper into the darker side of his sexual obsessions. I never dreamed how far he would go and to what depth he was so eagerly willing to travel.
Within four years after I left him, he would be dead because of his sexual obsession.

... hiding the horses ...

Trying to save the horses from Alfred would turn out to be a fulltime job for Bud and myself.

It all began shortly after I told Alfred that I wanted a divorce. I still had two mares with their foals at our older place and the girls had been looking after them for me for the last year.

I had traded "Mary," a dark bay thoroughbred broodmare that was expecting to foal that year, for a 3/4 truck from a friend in Grande Prairie named Kathy. Alfred had taken the only vehicle that I had to pull the horse trailer. He claimed he needed my truck for his job, even though I had bought him a Jimmy blazer for the purpose.

Faunus, my two year old colt, had been hauled to Edmonton to the vet already by a friend from High Level. She was on her way to the Vet Clinic outside of Edmonton with her mare and took Faunus with her. Faunus had to have surgery on his neck to remove the stick and was to be on stall rest until it healed.

I arranged with a friend in Camrose, named Cheryl, to lease my other broodmare, Velecka, a light bay thoroughbred brood mare for a year. She would look after Velecka's three month old filly, named, Whinny, until she was weaned.

Arrangements were made for Velecka to be hauled also to the veterinary facilities in Edmonton. From there, Cheryl would pick her and her foal up and move them to her place outside of Camrose. Cheryl was going to breed Velecka to her paint stallion and keep that foal, in exchange for boarding costs. When Whinny was to be weaned I would then move her to the same place that the rest of my horses were eventually headed, to Bashaw to Doug's farm. Everything was set or so I thought.

When it was time to move Velecka, Kathy had offered to haul her to Edmonton for me. Kathy was to arrive at the farm, and with Emily's help, load both Velecka and Whinny in to her trailer and leave for Edmonton. Sounds simple, right? Wrong.

When Kathy arrived at the house to pick up Velecka and Whinny, Wheezy came roaring out of her house shouting at Kathy that she was going to have her charged with theft if she took the mare and foal. Emily came out of our old house and heard all the noise from her grandmother, Wheezy. Emily stormed over to Kathy's horse trailer and screamed at her grandmother to shut up and go back into her house. Emily yelled at her that Velecka belonged to me. With her puffed up red face, Wheezy then asked Emily whose side she was on in the divorce. Emily screamed that she was not on anyone's side. Wheezy screamed back at Emily that she was taking my side and that she would be sorry.

The fight in the yard was not very pleasant. Kathy called me on the cell phone and told me what was happening in the yard. She said that she was afraid to take the horses to Edmonton. I told her that everything would be okay, just have Emily help load the horses and get out of there. Kathy said that the things that Wheezy was screaming to Emily were unbelievable. No grandmother should talk to her granddaughter that way.

Then Emily rushed into our house and phoned me on my cell phone and told me what was happening. She was furious with her grandmother.

I told Emily that I was still about 45 minutes away from the house. She knew that Bud and I had been in High Level working and were on route to our home town.

When Emily had run into our house, Wheezy seized the opportunity and ran into her house and phoned Alfred, to tell him that I was moving the horses. Apparently he instructed her to call the police and have Kathy arrested for theft.

After I had hung up the phone with Emily, I called Wheezy and Stan. They would not pick up the phone so I left them a message. I told them that they had better back off. I said that they knew the horses belonged to me and they should mind their f'ing own business for once and they had better leave the girls alone. Then I called Alfred on his cell and asked him "What in the hell do you think you are doing? We discussed leasing out Velecka and you agreed. Why did you change your mind? What is going on?"

His reply was, "I changed my mind and none of the horses are going anywhere. If they're moved, I'm going to charge that person with theft."

I shook my head and told him that he was unbelievable and disconnected the call.

Well, you guessed it. Wheezy was in her glory and promptly called the police to report the theft as her precious son had instructed.

Kathy and Emily had finished loading the two horses when Emily decided that she was travelling with the horses to make sure that they made it to Edmonton without any problems. Emily did not want Kathy charged by the police, and she did not trust what her grandmother would do.

Emily and Kathy had gone about a half a mile down our side road when a police car stopped them. The police officer told Emily and Kathy that he was going to have to charge them with theft, because they took horses off the property that they did not live on. Emily informed the officer that she lived on the farm and the horses belonged to her family. The police officer had to let them go.

Stupidity from Alfred and his parents was running rampant that day.

Once Emily and Kathy were on their way, next came the task of figuring out how to move Athena, a black 17 hand Trakhener mare with attitude and her foal. I did not have a truck to pull Dad's stock trailer, and Dad and Mom were not home to offer any help. Really I was not sure if Athena would have fit into the stock trailer anyway. I had no idea where Alfred was. I wasn't sure what to do, but I knew I had to quickly move my last two horses from Alfred's parents' land or risk never getting them back.

Since Bud and I had been in High Level on a business trip and we were both wearing our business clothes, him a suit and me a pair of dress slacks and top. We were not dressed to be mucking around on the farm.

When we finally arrived in town, Emily and Kathy were well on their way to Edmonton with Velecka and Whinny. The next thing that I had to worry about was Athena and her foal, Mac. How was I going to get her off the property and out of Wheezy's and Alfred's greedy clutches? There was no one around that could help me or wanted to help me. None of our old friends that lived in our small town wanted to suffer the wrath of Alfred.

Bud was not familiar with horses and really did not know anything about them or how to handle them. Sometimes being naïve is the best answer you need.

Bud was trying to help come up with a solution, but I was shooting down every one that he came up with. I was so frustrated and scared. My mind was closed off from everything except saving my horses. Finally Bud looked at me and said, "Why can't we lead them out of the yard and walk them to your parents' house?"

There were many reasons that I could come up with showing Bud that his plan would not work:

> One: my parent's place was over 10 miles away;
> Two: Athena's foal was not halter broken;
> Three: Athena was not actually a co-operative mare most of the time;

Four: Bud was not allowed on Alfred's parents' property, with him being the other guy and all according to Alfred's story about the marriage break up. So he could not help me bring them out;

Five: We had to cross a major highway and then walk along another major highway for 4 or 5 more miles before reaching my parents' place; and

Six: I had no idea where Alfred was hiding. He had said that he was heading to his parents' place but I did not know how far away he was or even if he was really coming at all. To me there were too many things that could go wrong.

I needed help but I did not want to ask Tasha to help after what had happened to Emily. I had no choice, so I went along with Bud's plan.

Tasha was nervous to be around Bud and me. It was very clear that she knew that her grandparents and her father would turn on her if they thought she was helping me in any way. She did not want to be involved in the divorce and I did not blame her in the least. Heck, I did not want to be involved in it either but I had no choice if I was ever going to have a normal life.

Alfred and his parents had planted the "seed of division" regarding their idea of loyalty in the girls' mind and this seed had started to grow. It seemed that they figured Emily was on my side and Tasha was on her father's side. Neither one of the girls, I am sure wanted to take anyone's side, they would have preferred to have both their parents, not one.

Tasha was the only one around that could have helped me remove Athena and Mac, but I was not going to ask her. Thank heavens Tasha offered to help lead them off the property. Bud was to stand on the side of the road with Tasha's vehicle, the trees would block him from Wheezy and Stan's sight. He would wait there for us to bring the mare and foal by the north side of our house, across the front lawn and down the driveway. I did not want Wheezy and Stan to see Bud was there and cause more problems, so Bud waited out of sight.

173

Walking onto Alfred's parents' property was not an easy task, but I could not let them know that I felt uncomfortable. I could not let Wheezy smell any fear, so I marched right down the middle of their driveway in between the two houses. Tasha came out of our house and walked with me straight to the back where the corrals were.

I don't know why his parents did not come out of their house and try and stop me. Maybe they knew better, since they both knew that the horses were mine in the first place. Wheezy obviously felt it was easier now to pick on her granddaughter then it was to pick on me.

When I reached the back corral where Athena was standing, my heart was racing. I had to hurry and get the horses before Alfred arrived. I was amazed that both horses stood there for us while Tasha and I put on the halters and even more surprised that Athena and Mac actually led quietly out of the yard without fighting us. Maybe Bud's plan was going to work after all.

Once the two horses were off the property, Tasha and I walked the horses a short ways down the road to meet up with Bud. Next came the task of leading the two horses over 10 miles. Tasha handed Athena's lead rope to Bud, but Athena was starting to become excited, so I thought it would be best if I led her and Bud followed with her foal. I had hoped that Mac would follow his mother and not cause Bud too much trouble. Tasha got into her vehicle and left.

Boy, was I wrong.

We had walked about ½ mile when Stan came zooming down the road in his pick-up truck, with dust and rocks flying everywhere. I believe that he was hoping to get the two horses to spook as he whipped past. Athena was being a handful already, whinnying and running around me in circles. She was excited because the terrain was unfamiliar to her and her pasture buddies were gone.

I knew that if Stan zoomed past, Athena would rear up and try to run back to the farm. Both horses could get hurt.

As Stan's truck came closer, I deliberately turned and walked Athena to the middle of the road. I told Bud to stay near the edge with Mac. As I continued leading her down the center, Stan was approaching us at a good clip. He was forced to slow down and drive partway in the ditch to get past me. I was hoping that he would not decide to run me over instead. Maybe he wasn't so stupid after all.

After Stan had passed, Mac decided that being led was not what he wanted to do anymore and he started to rear up or flop onto the ground in a tantrum. Poor Bud was at a loss as to what to do. When Mac could smell Bud's hesitation in handling him, he took full advantage of the situation. He started to run circles around Bud trying to get away from him. I led Athena back over to the ditch and handed her lead rope to Bud. I told him to continue leading Athena down the road. When I had taken Mac's lead rope from Bud I quickly grabbed hold of his halter to gain control of him. I continued to walk him down the road behind his mother. When he flopped on the ground, I kicked him to make him get back up and walk. I was in no mood for any more crap that day.

Mac's behaviour went on for about another mile. Finally both horses settled down for the rest of the long hot and dirty journey.

After we had gone three miles, we stopped to let Mac nurse. He was worn out from the fast pace we were travelling. When he was finished we continued on our way.

I am sure that the people passing us thought that we were crazy. All they saw were two people in business clothes leading two horses down the highway with no possible destination in sight.

Tasha, bless her heart, had caught up with us after we had crossed the major highway. She was making sure that we weren't having any trouble. Bud and I had been travelling at a good pace and were dying of thirst, so I sent her to town to buy Bud and me something to drink.

I don't think that either of us has ever walked and jogged a faster 10 mile marathon with two horses in tow. We managed to make it to Mom's and Dad's in two hours.

As far as I knew, I don't think Alfred went to his parents' place that day. I guess it was just another mind game of his.

When Alfred found out that I had gotten Athena and Mac off his parents' land he was furious. He demanded to know where they were. I never told him, but I am sure that my brother and his wife did. I knew that we had to hurry and move Athena and Mac off my parents' land and hide them someplace else. I did not want Alfred coming after them, although I was pretty sure that he would not try to lead Athena and Mac. He never really handled the horses, he was afraid of them.

When the horses were safely hidden in the back of Mom's and Dad's property, Bud and I got in his car and headed back to Camrose. The following weekend we would be back to move Athena and Mac to their temporary home in Bashaw.

I am still amazed that Bud had offered to help me move the horses that day. It tells you a lot about someone when they offer their help without expecting anything in return, especially when it involves something that they have no experience dealing with. That day and the following week when we had to move them again, Bud showed me his true colours.

... Joyous Noel, not so joyous ...

The first Christmas without my girls was the most horrible one in my life. Christmas was a big deal for us, the girls being born on Christmas Day just added to the special feeling during that time.

I was trying to make arrangements to see the girls on Christmas Day. Mom and Dad had gone to BC for the winter and I could not stay with any of my siblings. I was trying to get a hotel or motel room in our home town but there were not any rooms available. I was devastated.

Mom and Dad had invited Bud and I to go to BC to spend the holiday with them, I think they were missing their kids too during the holidays. That Christmas, the stress and missing the girls was too much for me. When we arrived at Mom's and Dad's place I was very sick and had to spend the next three days in bed.

When I called the girls on Christmas morning to wish them a "Happy Birthday" and "Merry Christmas," they asked me how Vegas was. I told the girls that I was not in Vegas and asked why they would think that I was.

Alfred had told the girls that I had preferred to spend Christmas with Bud in Las Vegas instead of with them.

I told them that I missed them and that I had tried to come to see them but I could not find a place to stay. I could barely keep it together while I talked to them, so Mom came to my rescue and took the phone from me and started talking to the girls and wishing them a Merry Christmas.

The long drive home a few days later was taxing to say the least, with poor Bud having to stop on the side of the mountains for me to be sick or go to the washroom in the snow.

... saving Arion ...

Arion was one of the warm-bloods that I had raised. He was a 16.2 hh Trakehner gelding. Arion was the most gorgeous dark bay with a black mane, tail and legs. His nostrils were lined with soft black hair and he had the most incredible deep brown eyes that held a hint of mischievous twinkle in them. Arion was my dream horse. When I started to compete Arion in his fifth year he would strut around like a peacock. He knew he was a handsome lad and he wanted everyone else to know it too. He loved to show off and hated it if he didn't win his class, and he would become a bit of handful when leaving the arena behind the winning horse or horses. He was my funny guy that way and I loved him for it.

Twice I had to carefully nurse Arion back to health, once in 1993 after he had pulled his front tendons when he was four years old, and again, in 1998, when he contracted pneumonia and nearly died. Bud and I spent hours grinding up and feeding him 150 pills a day at a cost of $3,000 for the month, money that I really didn't have.

The hours that Arion and I spent together during these uncertain times really deepened our bond.

I guess that is the difference that love and devotion can make. Arion was an anchor to my sanity and I was not about to let him die on me. I was not about to let Alfred destroy him.

During the second time of saving Arion, Alfred had kept up the financial and emotional pressure. He had refused to let me use my truck, – which was in his possession, to haul Arion to the vet. Alfred told me that he hoped that Arion died. If Arion died it would have been my fault because I had left him. He said that I was paying the price for my decision to end the marriage.

I knew that Alfred had gained control over the girls' minds about me, and that was something that haunted me every day, but I refused to let him try and destroy my horse too. That was something that I had control over. I did not know how I was going to pay for everything, but I did not care. I would make the money somehow, some way. I just had to take one day at a time and not look at that total amount that it was costing.

I thought to myself: *Close your eyes, breathe deep and take one day at a time.*

Later, after Arion had finished his yearlong rehab program, I moved him to a stable outside of Edmonton. We then started the long process of retraining for our dream to compete at the Canadian Dressage Nationals as partners.

This was the only thing Alfred could not take away from me, no matter how hard he tried: my dream.

The journey to the nationals was not going to be an easy one with no money but the only direction was up and nobody was going to stop me.

Over the next few years, Arion and I had become very successful in the Dressage ring, but all things come to an end.

My meagre resources had been slowly coming to an end. It had been difficult keeping Arion safe from Alfred and the cost of boarding and training was crippling. I had been counting on Alfred to pay the settlement from the divorce so that I could go to the Canadian Dressage Nationals. But it had been two years since the settlement had been awarded and Alfred still had not paid what he owed.

I was sitting at my kitchen table contemplating what to do next. *Should I go or not, can I afford the money to go or not?* I thought *there is always next year maybe, but I'm not sure if Arion can do another year of hard training.*

The many broken promises over the years from Alfred should have told me not to count on him for anything.

Little did I know that the 2000 Canadian Dressage Nationals was going to be our last competition ever.

To make a long story short, I was forced to sell Arion right after the Nationals for his safety. Arion and I did very well, under the circumstances, but it was bittersweet. At least Bud had been able to make it there is see our last competition. It was a heartbreaking for him as well as for me.

Alfred's refusal to pay the divorce settlement and his constant threatening to find Arion to shoot him had forced me to look after Arion's best interests and not mine. Alfred had won.

It was the day before Arion was to leave on the truck for Kentucky to go to his new owner. I had gone out to the barn to see him one last time and to say goodbye.

Arion knew that something was happening, I guess he could sense my frustration and devastation. Usually the minute he saw me he would nicker and come over and nuzzle me for a treat.

Today Arion did not come to see me. Instead he stood there looking at me with those big brown eyes, searching my face, looking for his own answers as to what was happening. I felt like a traitor, hell, I *was* a traitor and I could not bear the look on his beautiful face. So we both stood there staring at each other.
I could not believe that the last four years had come to this.

Finally I could not take it anymore, I walked over to Arion, gave him a hug, rubbed his head and whispered in his ear, "I'm so sorry, I love you."

Arion didn't acknowledge that I was even there; it appeared that according to him I was just someone; a nobody.
I was so devastated as I said my goodbye and turned to leave. Arion was mad at me and let me know it in no uncertain terms.

Just before I was fully out of his sight, I turned to have one last look at him. Arion had not taken his eyes off me as I was walking away. In that one brief moment as our eyes met, I saw the devastation and betrayal he was feeling. About a week after Arion had left for Kentucky I had to sign his papers over for the new owner. It was unbearable. I was totally devastated as my shaky hand tried to write my name. I just could not get over this feeling of loneliness. My partner was gone and now I had no one to go to and talk, the sanctuary was gone.

Over the years that I had poured out my feelings to him, Arion never interrupted me. He just patiently listened. I just couldn't believe it had come to this! I could no longer hold back the tears.

To this day I still miss him and can't stop the tears from flowing as I tell this story. He will remain in my heart and thoughts forever, for he was a true gift from God.

... a death, and a murder contract ...

It was after Alfred's unexpected death in Sept 2000 that I was forced to seek help in dealing with him, his death, the murder contract and his haunting me.

The shock of finding out that the man that I had been married to for 21 years would actually hire someone to kill me was surreal. After Alfred's unexpected death, the girls and I, along with my two brothers had driven the couple of hours from our old place to Alfred's rental house to move his stuff back to our old house where the girls were living. We could not find the landlord to open up the house so Emily and I headed to the police station to see if they could find him, while everyone else waited at the rental house in case the landlord finally did show up.

The lady constable kept looking at me with a strange expression and asked Emily and I if we would like to ask her anything regarding Alfred's death. Emily was starting to get very upset with this line of questioning and I was getting suspicious, so I asked Emily to go and wait in the car while I got things figured out with the landlord.

I sat in the police headquarters' private room listening to the constable explaining to me Alfred's intentions regarding me and the circumstances of his death. I was numb. I knew he had problems with his sex addition, but I would never have believed that Alfred had hired someone to kill me. All of the different scenarios that he had researched and regarded as my "just fate," and all of the kidnapping/ murder/suicide scenes that the police had found notes on were overwhelming.

Later that day, when I finally arrived back at my parents' farm, I told them what had happened with the landlord's refusal to allow us to remove Alfred's belongings and about Alfred's intentions to end my life and possibly the girls' lives as well. They could not believe it and Dad said to forget about it.

I thought to myself, *Forget about it? How in the hell am I supposed to forget about it? With Alfred dead at least, likely the girls' lives are safe but there still is a madman out there somewhere with a contract to kill me!*

I was so upset with them that I left the house and headed out in the back field where the large round bales were still sitting scattered throughout the field waiting to be picked up and stacked in the yard. I walked past several of the large bales and finally when I could not walk anymore because I was shaking too badly, I sat down behind one.

I was thinking to myself, the *girls have to deal with their father's cause of death, they do not need to know this bit of information too. They are already in shock.*

My mind had slowly been going numb sitting there on the cold ground. I could not move and I could not comprehend that my body was starting to go into shock from the knowledge I had just learned. The only rational thought that persisted was, *"how am I going to survive this one?"*

I had no idea who this person was and when this person was going to kill me.

Well, as you can see, I did survive that also. It was a hard road at times but without Alfred funding the contract and the police investigation into the hired gun, at least that part was dealt with. The next thing Alfred did was going to take a lot longer.

... seeking help ...

I used to think that when someone died, that was it, they left this earth and went to heaven or to hell, depending on the life they lived. I would soon realize that Alfred did not go anywhere that he was supposed to go.

Now, most of you will think that she had finally lost it; the girl had gone "cuckoo, nuts, whacko." I thought that maybe I had lost it too. Maybe I finally had been pushed over that precipitous edge that I had been balancing on for so long. Alfred's untimely death due to his sex obsession had shocked his parents, his siblings, his girls and definitely me.

Since Alfred did not know where I lived in life, it was surprising to me that he would find me in his death, but he did. And then all hell broke loose. I thought that I was never going to escape him, so I went to my doctor and told her that I was having problems dealing with Alfred's death and what I thought was also going on. I figured my doctor would admit me into the "nut house" with this one, but instead Dr. Brooks referred me to Lorraine Nicely, a pastoral care counsellor. When I started to see Lorraine I was only seeking help to deal with Alfred and with what all that encompassed, but little did I know that everything else that had happened in my life was about to come boiling to the surface.

Over the course of the next several months, I had weekly visits with Lorraine. It did not take long for her to realize that this was not just about Alfred but so much more. Lorraine started to dig deeper into my past.

Pandora's Box was getting cracked open and I did not like it.

By the time we had finished all of our sessions over the next few years, my life had travelled a full circle working backwards. I started to relive some of the most traumatic and horrifying events that I had refused to acknowledge. Even though I knew of their existence, I did not want to relive them. But I knew that until I did I would never have peace. Maybe God had finally sent me my "peacemaker."

My talks with Lorraine started off first with discussions about the divorce and Alfred's behaviour and his death. I talked about our marriage and what had happened over the 21 years we had been husband and wife. I told her about his possessiveness and anger and jealousy toward other men.

I talked about when we would go out to social dances, and how Alfred would guard me like a watchdog. If someone came up to me to ask me to dance, Alfred would glare at him and the guy would leave. In time, word got around and pretty soon Alfred and I would be alone at the dance.

No one dared to come over because of him. I loved to dance and over the years, Alfred would allow a few older farmers, my relatives and a few good friends of his to dance with me. I guess Alfred did not see them as a threat.

During these years, I was unaware of the scenes that were happening behind my back. Alfred was always careful to never let me see him glaring at anyone and he never told me about the special little chats he had with the guys that had dared to ignore his glares.

Lorraine asked me about the divorce and what had happened during it regarding Alfred's possessiveness. I told her that he made one comment to me when we were getting the divorce. He said, "Okay, but you cannot see anyone else. You can only have sex with me when I come here."

I told her that I said, "That is not a divorce and you and I will not be having sex and I can see whomever I want, if I chose to." I told her that Alfred immediately asked me if there was someone else in the picture. I told him, "No, there is no one else, I don't want another relationship. I am not interested in having sex with anyone."

I said that Alfred seemed fine with the separation, he went about his life and I mine. It appeared that we could be friends during this time. But then he started to constantly keep tabs on me. He would start phoning around 10:00 pm and would continue until I got home from the stable which was around midnight. When I got home and answered the phone, Alfred would be on the other end, mad. He would start to question me on my whereabouts. When I told him that I had been at the stable riding he would then quiz me as to why I was so late. I told Lorraine that this type of conversation and behaviour went on for months until I changed jobs and was able to ride the three horses during the day and work at night with clients. My insurance appointments never lasted past 9:00 pm, so I was always home before 10:00 pm when he would start calling.

I told her that the pressure from Alfred's constant inquisitions and innuendos had started to psychologically affect me. I had no appetite, I did not sleep and I hated to go home to all the phone messages he had started to leave on my phone.

When I finally told Lorraine about the noises and feelings that I was experiencing in our apartment, I was relieved when she didn't have me committed to the "nut house."

Lorraine helped me realize that there are things in the world that happen to you and you need to have faith to get through it.

When we were finished dealing with Alfred, Lorraine honed in on comments that I had made during our conversations about abuse.

I remember making the comment that maybe it was my fault that Alfred regarded me as a sex object because I probably exuded that

187

type of energy. I had started to feel that way because, in my brain, it had already happened several times before. I didn't think that I was sending out the "abuse me and rape me" energy, but maybe I was. After all, if I wasn't, why did Alfred do what he did to me during our marriage when I had trusted him? I thought that maybe it was my fate in life.

I told Lorraine that I did not want to be someone's sex object. If having a relationship meant that, then I did not want to have any man in my life. I was afraid that if I had another relationship, then he would become like the rest.

When Lorraine finally got me to start talking about Ted, I told her that it had happened three times but I could not remember the third attack. I also told her that I was abused by a family member but could not really remember any details. The only clue that I had was a mini snapshot of me laying on my back and the family member on top of me.

Lorraine asked me who it was, but I refused to tell her. I said that I was afraid to say who because for years I kept telling myself it was a "memory transfer" from Ted to the family member.

That was the explanation that I had given myself so that I would not have to deal with it. I don't even know if there is such a thing as a "memory transfer" from one abuser to another. But the excuse, I think kept me sane until I was ready to deal with it.

Loraine then asked me, "Are you sure it did not happen with the family member?"

For years I had refused to think about it. I didn't want to believe that a trusted family member would or could do that to me when I was only five or six. Sitting in front of Lorraine, once again I refused to believe it, even though that little voice was nagging at me, telling me to remember the image and to trust myself.

During the next several sessions, Lorraine wanted me to think back and describe to her the first attack with Ted. I was to tell her in detail what was playing in my mind.

On the first attempt to relive the memory, I recalled:
I was drying dishes; no one was in the house. Ted came in and sat on the couch with his legs spread apart. He told me to come over and touch his thing. He was holding it in his hand.
I said, "No!"
The next thing I remember is Ted is holding me and he is making me touch his thing.
I was scared and crying lying on the floor.
I got up and finished drying the dishes.

I sat there looking at Lorraine. My mouth had gone dry. I tried to swallow but couldn't. I managed to say to her, "That is all I remember."

She suggested that I do some deep breathing and then go back and see if I could remember anything else. She wanted me to begin at the beginning again and tell her what I saw. I told her the same memories.

I was obviously suppressing the full memory, so Lorraine decided that with REM (rapid eye movement) therapy I should be able to release more of the suppressed memories.

Each time that she performed REM more of the memory came forward. After each of these sessions not only was I mentally and physically exhausted but I was also horrified yet relieved at the same time when I finally allowed myself to remember all of the first attack.

I remembered the colour of my clothes, his clothes, his smell and everything that was said. Every detail was filled in living colour. Not only was my mind reliving that moment in time, but so was my body. Once more I was that five year little girl and once more I felt the weight of the world on my tiny shoulders.

Ted was going to hurt and kill my Mom and Dad if I told anyone what he had done.

During each session we talked about how I was feeling and how I felt during and after the reliving of the memory. At the end of the session, Lorraine had me repeat some very important positive things that I was feeling about myself at that moment before ending the REM therapy.

REM is called "Rapid Eye Movement" therapy, how it works is your eyes follow the counselor's hand back and forth, similar to the swinging pendulum of a clock. This eye movement helps release the subconscious so the memories can be recalled that have been suppressed due to trauma. If you hit a stumbling block when you are trying to recall the memory, then the REM is repeated after you have taken a few deep cleansing breaths.

During REM you must concentrate on getting the memory to come alive and trust that what you are seeing is true. When my memories were returning from the fog, it seemed like I was watching a video clip in my head.

The release of these memories will help take the charge off them, and the memories will slowly go back into your childhood were they belong and hopefully be forgotten. If they can't be forgotten, then at least when you think about them, which you don't anymore, there are no more emotions and physical reactions attached to them. These traumatic memories will become like all the other memories that you can recall from your past, but now your heart does not race because of them.

During our REM sessions, Lorraine would constantly have to ask me to repeat to her what I was seeing. There were many times that I could not say out loud what my mind was reliving and playing back for me. The scenes were too graphic and the numbing pain too real to put into words.

At the same time period that I had started doing the REM sessions with Lorraine, both Emily and I were in an Entrepreneur Program designed to help people to start their own business. We were two months in the program when the program instructor told everyone in the class that we had to write a story. The theme of the story was to be: "What we think made us the way we are today."

Now talk about divine intervention on this story. Someone upstairs was definitely having a little control over that topic.

On my next visit to see Lorraine, I told her that I was going to write about the abuse from Ted. She was concerned that I was not fully ready to relive that experience in front of other people.

I figured that the charge of the memory was now off and I would be able to read the story out loud and not have a problem. For years I had lived with the memory, and if I wanted to put that part of my life behind me, I had to do it. I had to face down that demon in front of a room full of people that I had known for less than two months.

When I was finished writing that story, I tried to read it out loud to myself. I was surprised to hear my voice crack and that I could not finish it. After several more attempts to read it, I finally was able to get through it all. Next came the challenge of reading it out loud in front of Bud. Again my voice was cracking but now the tears were flowing. I forced myself to finish the story and not stop. When I was done, I asked Bud not to say a word. The look on his face was enough.

I did not want him to hug me or touch me; I did not want his pity. This was my battle and I felt that I did not want him or anyone else to feel sorry for me because of what had happened. I did not want this to have any control over me or anyone else again. I had not re-lived the memory in order to get pity or sympathy. I had re-lived it to free myself.

The overwhelming need for Bud to protect me from all of the pain of the memories was difficult for him. He had to figure out how to stand beside me and support me without showing his own disgust and raw emotions when hearing the details. I could not handle his pain from hearing about the events as well as my own for reliving them on this terrifying journey to find peace for my soul.

A few days later it was time to stand up in front of the class and read our stories. When it was my turn, I was not expecting anything to happen. After all I had reread that story quite a few times, so to my way of thinking the emotional charge should be getting less or off all together. When I walked up and stood behind the podium the tears were already streaming down my cheeks and I could not find my voice. One of the instructors asked me if I would like to do my story some other time. I looked at her and said, "No." Then I quietly asked everyone in the room to just ignore the tears and my runny nose, that I would be fine. As I read that story, the tears continued to fall, my nose never stopped running, my voice was cracking, but I did it. I finished it and for the first time in my life I felt like I had started to remove some of the weight off my shoulders.

It did not matter to me whether these people believed me or not, what mattered was that I believed me.

... "oh my God" it's really true ...

My sessions with Lorraine continued on for about a year. It was a year full of events that were helping me put the past behind me and allowing me to appreciate who I was. I started to understand much more where I had come from.

When I figured that I didn't need Lorraine anymore, I quit going for our weekly visits. I still had not talked about the family member that had raped me. I still had not said his name out loud. I did not want to believe that it was true. The illusions and excuses that I had always told myself for nearly forty years would come crashing down in the following year.

I cannot describe to you the feeling that you get when you find out that what you had been dreading all of your life, was actually true. The full impact of this knowledge was devastating for me.

I finally knew for sure, that the mini image that had played in my mind every time I had seen him over the past 30 years was real.

No longer did I think I was losing my mind, and no longer did I not believe that little girl inside of me. For decades that little girl had begged me to believe in her.

Once more another closure and a new beginning was about to start for me.

It was May of 2002, and Hank and Edna were celebrating their 25th wedding anniversary. I was standing in the kitchen of my parents' house. Everyone was getting ready for the evening's event. Mom was so happy, she turned to look at me and said, "At least one of my children made it to 25 years of marriage."

I stood there feeling like a failure again, it was as if that comment was another low blow to my inability to function normally. I had let her down again. It did not matter to her that I could not continue to stay in my marriage with any hopes of a normal life. Maybe to my Mom, I was a loser, a quitter and a disgrace, but call me what you want. I knew in my heart and soul that I was a survivor.

I was still searching for a "normal life." I knew one was out there somewhere. Then again, maybe I was in one now with Bud. What is normal? I had no clue.

It was the day after the anniversary party and everyone was at the farm. Edna walked over to me and said that she liked the outfit I was wearing and she wanted to know if there were any more left in the store where I was working. I told her that there were, and asked her what size she took. Edna asked to try on the pants that I was wearing to see how they fit her so that she would know what size she would take.

So we headed off to the bathroom so that I could slip of my pants and let her try them on. While we were in the bathroom Edna asked me if I remembered anything happening in my childhood with Nelson.

I could feel the color draining from my face: my mind was whirling and went instantly back to the scene of me lying on the bed with him on top of me. Thoughts were forming in my mind:

Did that bastard do something to Hank too?
Had he hurt Hank?
Was it all true?

Not willing to trust Edna and her motives, I forced myself to ask her, "Why, did something happen to Hank?"

She replied: "No, it happened to you."

My mouth was dry and my breathing had gotten shallow. My mind has suddenly realized, that the image was true.

I had never told a soul about the image I kept having every time I saw Nelson.

It was true, it had happened.

When I gained control of my breathing, I looked at her and said, "What do you mean?"

She said, "Hank remembers Nelson did something to you when you were little." She asked again, "Do you remember anything?"

Edna said "That is why Hank did not want Nelson at our 25th wedding anniversary, because he had done something to you." She pressed me again, "Did he?"

I was always very cautious about anything I said to Edna and this time was no exception. I said, "What does he remember?"

She said "Hank remembers Nelson coming into the house and telling him and Al to go outside. Nelson made you stay in the house with him. Hank snuck back into the house to see what was going on. He saw Nelson with you in their bedroom."

I did not want to confirm or deny anything with Edna. I wanted to figure out if she was talking about that same image I kept having about Nelson.

I told her, "Yes, something had happened." I never did tell her what had happened that day.

Within the hour Bud and I left the farm to drive back home. On the four hour trip home I finally told Bud about Nelson and what I remembered.

I called Lorraine the next day and made an appointment.

In time, as these new sessions progressed, Lorraine said that I had to confront Nelson somehow to fully deal with the memory. I had to let him know that I remembered what he had done to that little five or six year old girl.

I told Lorraine that I did not want to see him, I did not want to confront him. I only wanted the memory to go away.

Lorraine said that the family secret was destroying my family and if I wanted to fully heal then I had to tell them all about the secret. I told her that I was afraid that no one would believe me. I knew I had lost that argument when she reminded me that I was not the only one that remembered what had happened to me. Hank remembered too.

I guess I hoped, because Hank was Mom's favourite, that she would not have any choice but to believe me.

Several months later I gathered up my courage and called Hank and asked him what he remembered about Nelson. He said that he couldn't remembered anything. All he said was that he remembers that Nelson told him and Al to go outside and that I had to stay in the house with Nelson. Hank said that he later came back into the house, and that both Nelson and I were gone. He then said he went into the bedroom and noticed something dark on the bed. He thought it was poop.

He knew something was not right.

Hank said the three of us kids were not very old at the time and shortly after that Nelson left.

Hank then said that he never seen anything, and does not remember anything about his childhood.

Hank did not remember Ted working for Dad, but I know that Ted did work for Dad because they had confirmed it when I told them that he had molested me. At the time Ted and Nelson were close friends.

As Hank talked to me, it sounded like he had seen more that he was willing to tell me. Maybe he had suppressed most to his memory also, because of what he said he had seen. I thought, *too many things don't make sense.*

I wondered, *if Hank only saw what he says is "poop" on the bed, why would he think something terrible had happened to me?*

I know that he saw something horrible, which probably caused him to suppress his memory and to forget his childhood. Believe me, I know what that is like. I know his memory will only start to surface if he allows it to. When that happens then he will be able to deal with those memories, if he wants to have peace. To this day he has chosen not to remember.

It was September and four months had passed since I had learned the truth about Nelson. Lorraine had been insisting that I had to tell the "secret" to my parents. Once again I was being put in the position of telling people that I loved that things were not as they seemed. That there was a secret that they had to know about.

I flashed back to the day I was forced by the police to tell my daughters the truth about their father's death and his pastime hobbies and I was not looking forward to telling this secret either.

I hated wasting another minute of my life dealing with what Nelson had done to me, and I hated having to tell everyone in my family about it. But deep down I knew that I had to if I was ever going to be free again.

I told Lorraine that I still did not want to see Nelson or even hear his voice, so I decided that I would write him a short note that simply read:

> "I remember what you did to me when I was five.
> You raped and molested me.
> I remember everything."

I knew the following day I was going to have to bite the bullet and mail that note to him. I marked the outside of the envelope "PRIVATE AND CONFIDENTIAL."

About a week after I sent the note to Nelson, I headed up north to the farm to tell my parents what had happened to me regarding Ted and Nelson when I was a child.

I asked them to come down to their bedroom as I had something important to tell them. After I told them about Ted and Nelson, my Dad asked me, "Why didn't you tell us?"

I looked at them and said, "I was five and scared, but I'm telling you now."

Dad said "I would have killed Ted if I'd known what he did to you." He also said, "Maybe, if we'd known about Ted, then Nelson would not have done what he did."

Dad could not sit there anymore on the bed, he got up and left. Mom sat there with tears in her eyes. She told me that Edna had already told her that Nelson had done something to me.

I was surprised but not shocked that Edna could not keep her big mouth shut about it. She always loved to gossip and since her and Hank were already fighting with Nelson regarding Dad's farm, I guess she figured that she would make sure that Mom was still on their side. What better way to cause more division in the family then to tell Mom that her favorite son, Hank had seen Nelson do something to me. To me, Edna and probably Hank were using what had happened to me as their own personal weapon of destruction regarding the farm and who will inherit it one day.

I knew that Hank had remembered more than he was telling me, and he told Edna. Why else would Edna have told Mom anything? Especially if she did not know what had really happened.

I knew that Hank was traumatized by the event also. He had only been 8 or 9 years old when it happened. I don't know why he never told Mom and Dad about it that night when it happened.

At the time of writing this book, it has been two years since Nelson received the note. I have not heard one word from him. I do know that he did get it, because I was told that whenever someone in my family mentions my name he goes berserk. I think he is afraid of what I might do next.

I think I'll just let him live with that for a while because I'm in no hurry to help him deal with his demons.

Since telling my parents about what Ted and Nelson had done to me, I noticed a definite change in the way they see me. No longer do they look at me with puzzlement. For my mom, I think it may have given her some encouragement, for she told me what had happened to her when she was also a child.

Mom and Dad never really knew who their oldest daughter was, they had been robbed of my life by two abusers that they knew very well and had helped and trusted.

I can't even comprehend the disappointment they must have felt when they found out about Nelson's violent behavior. The mixed emotions they must have for Nelson, Hank and myself must be in such a turmoil. They discovered that three of their family members were not who they thought they were.

I only know that my relationship with my parents has changed for the better. I guess a little understanding goes a long way.

For me, finally putting an end to it all and putting the past back in the past where it belongs has taken a long time.

This journey has been full of heartache, desperation, loneliness, isolation, anger, hatred, misunderstanding and frustration. My body reacted like it was happening all over: once again I suffered from infections, severe muscle pains and more, as I had to relive the abuse.

I can't change what happened to me, but I can confront the abuse and deal with it, then move on. I know that if I do not confront it and deal with it, it will always control my life.

If I did not deal with the abuse, then every decision that I made would continue to be a product of the abuse. I had to take control of my life. I had to take my power back from the abusers.

There were so many times that I wished the memories would simply go away on their own, but that never would happen. My decision making abilities had been greatly affected. I made life decisions based on the abuse and how it made me feel about myself. Decisions were made in my life, as I was fighting to protect myself from further abuse. All of the abuse-altered decisions I made started to be made at a very young age.

The abuse had a stranglehold on my soul, and in order to free myself I had to face the demons head on. Several times the demons may have won the battle but I eventually did win the war.

The feelings I have today are of peace. I have never felt so alive. The world looks different to me now. I notice more beautiful things around me.

I suddenly realize that I can hear birds singing, and for the first time in my life I am free!

EPILOGUE

I cannot begin to explain how it felt to be totally alone in a family, to feel that there is no one that you could count on. To feel that your existence did not matter.

In my family, the way things were dealt with, was to ignore them, never mention it again, never ask for help, and never admit that you needed help. As Mom always would say, "You have to deal with things yourself." That statement came from Mom's own childhood experience of abuse; that was how she handled it. Mom may have told her mother, I am not sure, but I do know she never dealt with it. I am sure she hoped, like many other victims of abuse, that it would go away. Mom's motto for the abuse was, "Just let sleeping dogs lie."

For me, the abuse and pain never went away on its own no matter how much I tried to ignore it.

I could not let sleeping dogs lie, for those dogs were eating me alive. They had continued to rob me of my life; they already had robbed me of my childhood, my youth, my teenage years and they were still robbing me of my adult life.

I couldn't change what happened to me, but I could confront the abuse and deal with it, then I could move past it. I knew that if I did not confront the abuse and deal with it, the abuse would always control my life and the decisions I made would be based on the abuse and how I felt about myself and others.

I decided that there was no way in hell I was going to give my abusers the rest of my life. I wanted to make something positive come out of this mess and tell my story in the hopes that other victims will also find their voices. I knew that I had to break the cycle of abuse and the cycle of silence.

I have realized many things on this past journey; the most important thing that I recognized was my spiritual side.

Throughout my life I've called on my spirituality to help me cope. My guardian angels, (and there were a few) have been with me always. They never left my side. At the toughest times when I was ready to give up, there were many helping hands to help me handle it all. My angels, the saints and the good Lord were there to comfort and console me.

I have realized that I trusted them and leaned on them for strength. Today, I take time to listen to their wisdom and trust my inner voice, for it was and is them talking to me and guiding me.

Please take time to notice abuse in a child or your own family. A person just does not change overnight into someone you do not know. There is a reason for this abrupt change. Look for signs in their behaviour, like a person suddenly becoming shy and withdrawn, or the opposite, aggressive and/or angry. Listen to what they are saying and what types of questions they are suddenly asking you. The questions may be about things that they should not have any knowledge of at their age.

If you question them, be kind in your words and tone, and above all be patient. Do not expect the child/person to tell you what has happened right away. You have no idea what has been said to them to force them to keep quiet. Seek help and guidance for them immediately, if you think something may have happened but are not sure what has happened. Talk to someone that you trust, your family doctor, minister, counsellor etc. Err on the side of caution for that person's sake.

If the abuse happened to you, perhaps a long time ago, and you are trying to figure out what is wrong with your life and why you are making incorrect decisions, start by asking yourself questions such as: "Why? What are my memories?" Ask someone that you trust like your family doctor, a priest, a friend, your family or a counsellor to help you to see if there is anything that you may be supressing in your subconscious. The most important thing I can say to you is believe what your memories are and deal with them.

You have the power to take back your life from your abuser/s. You cannot let the abusers define who you are or how you live your life. Only you have that power and that control.

Having a professional to talk to about your life choices and decisions will help you get on the right path.

My journey has been terrifying and disturbing but also very liberating, I am forever thankful for the people that took the time to notice and help me on my path to freedom.

I wish you joy and success in finding your right path and becoming a true survivor.

ABOUT THE AUTHOR:

Brenda and her husband Bud, live on a small farm outside of Edmonton, Alberta. Brenda continues to enjoy horses in her life, along with their two small dogs and a few cats. They have a successful insurance business and enjoy time with their five children and their grandchildren.

39284296R00122

Made in the USA
Charleston, SC
04 March 2015